MOVING AND LIVING
ABROAD

MOVING AND LIVING ABROAD
A Complete Handbook for Families

Sandra Albright
Alice Chu
Lori Austin

Revised By
Sandra Albright
Chase de Kay Wilson

HIPPOCRENE BOOKS
New York

For information, address: Hippocrene Books, 171 Madison Avenue, New York, NY 10016.

Library of Congress Cataloging-in-Publication Data

Albright, Sandra.
    Moving and living abroad: a complete handbook for families/ Sandra Albright, Alice Chu, Lori Austin; revised by Sandra Albright, Chase de Kay Wilson.
        p. cm.
    Includes index.
    ISBN 0-7818-0048-X (pbk.) : $14.95
    1. Americans—Employment—Foreign countries— Handbooks, manuals, etc. 2. Corporations, American— Employees—Relocation—Handbooks, manuals, etc. 3. Women—Employment—Foreign countries—Handbooks, manuals, etc. 4. Intercultural communication—Handbooks, manuals, etc. I. Chu, Alice. II. Austin, Lori. III. Wilson, Chase de Kay. IV. Title.
HF5549.5.E45A44 1992
640—dc20   92-26127
                                                        CIP

This book is dedicated to those women
and their families
who traveled our path before us and with us,
and who will do so after us.

Contents

Acknowledgments

ALTHOUGH CONCEIVED BY THREE AUTHORS, *Moving and Living Abroad* has truly been nurtured by many more. We wish to express our gratitude to the hundreds of expatriate wives around the world who took the time to share their years of experience with us so that others might benefit.

Most importantly, we would like to acknowledge the exceptional efforts of Chase Wilson, whose skill as an editor, patience as a friend and indomitable perseverance made that which was conceived a reality.

Foreword

WITH ABOUT THREE MILLION AMERICANS living abroad, an enormous subculture exists which has been relatively ignored in literature and the media. The adaptation of this expatriate group to its foreign environment is a critical element in the success or failure of U.S. business overseas.

Corporations spend significant time, effort, and money to assure effective selection and training of the people, mostly men, chosen to manage their international operations. Given the fact that most expatriate employees are men, their wives play a fundamental role in the success or failure of the expatriate experience. Yet the executive's wife, who performs the critical role of establishing and maintaining the family unit, is frequently forgotten. Most companies will candidly admit that if the wife fails, her husband is also likely to fail. If the wife is unprepared to cope or unable to adapt, the resulting destabilization of the family can have serious business consequences.

Despite the importance of the expatriate wife's role, few corporations are adequately prepared to counsel and assist the expatriate wife. It's not that a policy exists against such activities. Many companies simply do not have the necessary experience, expertise, or resources on staff.

The basic aim of *Moving and Living Abroad* is to assist in the preparation of the expatriate wife and family. The handbook will also assist unmarried expatriates, both male and female. This handbook has been written from the expatriate wife's unique perspective and focuses on the critical issues she will confront: first, in anticipation of an overseas assignment; and second, in adapting once her family is situated. Unlike available literature and travel guides, this book probes deeply into both the joys and frustrations of establishing a new life style in a foreign locale. The book also addresses the issue of jobs for women abroad after the expatriate family has settled into its new home. Although this handbook has been written with the expatriate wife in mind, it is a tool for all people who are or will be expatriates.

For the novice about to be transferred overseas, this handbook will serve as a primer on what to anticipate, identifying the "do's and don'ts" of managing the transition and explaining how to maximize the benefits of a foreign assignment. For the veteran expatriate wife, *Moving and Living Abroad* will serve as a refresher course on the prospects and pitfalls of living overseas, using the experiences of other seasoned pros.

With thirty years of international experience among them, the authors are eminently qualified to address the complex, sometimes sensitive, subject of moving and living abroad. As expatriate wives themselves, they experienced the problems and opportunities first-hand. Also, to supplement their own experiences, more than three hundred expatriates were polled by means of in-depth questionnaires and personal interviews and the resulting information was used by the authors in writing this book. The expatriate wives who were polled ranged in age from early twenties to mid-sixties; the expatriate children, from six to nineteen; and their families had experienced from one to twenty-five moves.

The book begins with an examination of one of the

most critical decisions a family may ever make—the decision of accepting or declining an overseas assignment. The book also reviews the advantages and necessity of a candid dialogue with an often untapped resource—the company. Then the move itself is examined—an event which without planning and preparation can prove to be the most traumatic and stressful experience in the entire process of living abroad. Culture shock, an often discussed but little understood phenomenon, is also explored in detail, as well as such fundamental issues as the rearing and education of children in a foreign location, personal safety, security, and sanitation. Other topics interwoven into the fabric of living overseas and discussed in this handbook are: functioning in and learning a foreign language; finding, training, and keeping household help; and finding work or otherwise combatting boredom after the overseas living pattern has been established.

The fundamental tenet of *Moving and Living Abroad* is the authors' firm conviction that the expatriate wife performs a critical role in establishing and maintaining the family unit in a foreign environment. If she fails or is unable to adapt, there is a high probability that the employee will fail as well. Conversely, if she is adequately prepared, knows what to expect, and benefits from the experience of other expatriate wives, her probability of successfully navigating the rapids of international life is excellent. The rewards of creating a stable, supportive environment at home and capitalizing on the unique cultural and educational opportunities of living abroad are outstanding— and well worth the effort. The objective of *Moving and Living Abroad* is to help the expatriate wife and her family to succeed.

Rather than cover the subject of moving to and living in any one particular country, the authors cover all subjects that would be common to almost all international moves.

The authors' aim is to give the expatriate wife and family a foundation, a beginning, and a helping hand as they begin their expatriate careers.

Throughout each chapter are the words of women who have faced the same problems, the same challenges, and the same rewards that any potential expatriate wife is about to face. It is hoped that this insight will help make the transfer as exciting, efficient, and painless as possible by providing the warnings, solutions, wisdom, and humor that have been developed over the years by experienced international wives.

PART ONE

CHAPTER I

Why People Move

DESPITE THE FACT THAT WE LIVE in the space age, man hasn't significantly changed his behavior patterns over the past hundreds of years. The driving forces of his life remain his social, economic, and psychological interdependency with his wife, family, and occupational environment. One of the key dynamics in this relationship is location—often raising the questions of: When and why does a man choose to move? What is he searching for and what does he hope to gain? Every man and every family will have their own unique answers to these questions. No two are ever likely to be the same.

The average American family moves once every four years. For the majority, relocation takes place within the boundaries of the United States. However, a significant percentage of the population opts for international relocation—to a new land, a new culture, and a new language. These people are characteristically more adventuresome, exploratory, and expansive. The men tend to be managers, professionals, and technicians—moving on behalf of large corporate organizations, foundations, or governmental institutions. Their wives come from all social, cultural, and

3

economic strata. However, the one thing these women all have in common is that they are *expatriate wives.* As such, they are a group in themselves and, while far from stereotypical, they all confront the same dynamics of international life.

What Are the Reasons for Moving?

Obviously there is no single answer to this question for all people. Nor is there usually a single, simple reason for any individual family. However, there do tend to be several key factors that influence the decision: survival, boredom, and life style.

Clearly, survival is one of the major reasons for migration. For many, psychological survival is as important a factor as economic and physical considerations. Stress and its causes tend to precipitate one of two reactions: total inactivity, or activity that will eventually allow the individual to solve his or her problems. This activity may not always be rational, but often the activity results in a change of venue. Those who have been burdened by family pressures, job pressures, advancing age, or societal prejudices have discovered that relocation is an ideal response.

For some people, movement is a fountain of youth. Movement represents an answer to their boredom—be it with themselves, their families, friends, business associates, or environs. Life overseas offers excitement, new challenges, and a chance for new directions. For some, it is a simple case of being restless by nature. Whether it is innate, inherited, or learned, no one can deny that some of us just have a yearning to move, to move again, and to keep on moving.

Believe it or not, I was bored in the States. Sure, it's

my native land and I would never change my citizenship, but suburbia holds no appeal for me. I didn't enjoy shoveling the snow in the winter, fertilizing the lawn in the spring, or passing my days at neighborhood coffee klatches. I didn't want to keep up with the Joneses. I wanted something new, exciting, different.

The opportunities for expanded cultural horizons afforded by living overseas are also alluring. Such a move promotes the acquisition of a new language and cultivation of new friends with diverse ethnic backgrounds. Hand in hand with living abroad is the opportunity to fulfill one's fantasies for travel, glamour, excitement, and adventure, virtually at the expense of someone else. What could be better?

We are both in our thirties and we own several houses and a couple of condominiums. We take lengthy vacations, stay at the best hotels, eat in the finest restaurants, and have accumulated many fine pieces of art work—all because we chose to live overseas. When we married we were in debt. Our financial future looked dismal at best. But now all that has changed. Sure there are drawbacks to living overseas, and I have no idea when we'll ever live in our dream house in the States, but at least I now know I'll have that dream house.

For many people the prospect of a better life style is the incentive. A move may result in extra funds, which can provide better schooling for the children and the opportunity to have household help and ensure the eventual purchase of the family's "dream house." Such moves can often result in the husband spending less time away from his family and a greater chance for close relationships among family members.

> I went because we had our children exactly one year apart. Therefore, we are looking forward to four children in college at the same time. There is no way that we could come up with the sufficient funds if we remained in the States, even if I worked. But, with the fringe benefits we receive by living abroad—company car, housing, and federal income tax deductions—not only can we put our children through university, we can live comfortably at the same time.

What's in It for the Wife?

A wife's reasons for making an overseas move may be the same as those of her husband. For some wives the sole purpose of an overseas move is to acquire sufficient financial reserves to fulfill a dream. For other women, life in the States has lost its meaning, or life abroad may appear to hold the key to solving personal or professional problems.

> My husband is a highly skilled technician, but unfortunately he chose a field where the supply for his talents was far more than the demand. We really didn't have much of a choice; we had to move to places where he could obtain work.

For others the transfer may offer an escape from domineering in-laws.

> Our parents were forever interfering in our marriage. Neither set seemed to believe that we knew how to take responsibility for our own lives or raise

our children. We literally couldn't wait to put the distance between us and them. We love our families, but the love we have for each other and our children is more important.

Some women may have worked to help maintain the family's financial health, and they may recognize that life abroad may ease the total financial burden on the family. Of course, there are women who want to work, who have successful careers in the States, and for whom the prospect of not working is most distressing. The choices that such women must make, to move or not, to subordinate their own careers in favor of those of their husbands, to change their own courses in midstream, are personal decisions—with numerous options, avenues, and directions to be considered.

Then, of course, there are those women who love to travel, who love to learn about other cultures and who want to be able to converse in more than one language. These women look upon international living as an opportunity to experience all that life has to offer as well as an opportunity to broaden their personal horizons and those of their children.

We had always lived in a small rural community, so moving abroad was a real eye opener for us all. Our children had never seen poverty and had never been exposed to different nationalities or religious customs and beliefs. TV and shopping malls were some of the things they believed existed everywhere, all over the world.

We don't miss TV and malls, and living in and learning about another culture has been more broadening than we anticipated. Imagine your child participating in a school's mock U.N. exercise with many of the "country representatives" really being from the designated country!

Status and prestige are also inducements for many women who, in their original communities, may have thought of themselves as just "little frogs in a big pond." Unlike her position in the States, where she may be but one of many company wives, she will most likely be perceived as closely associated with the company. Overseas, she will be part of the international community and may even become a leader of it. By moving she is likely to become more visible, not only as an ally to her husband and the company, but also as an individual.

The impetus to moving for some women is the opportunity to rise in society. The international wife may well dine with kings, millionaires, and dignitaries—none of which would have been possible had she remained at home.

The most important point is that, regardless of a wife's reasons for agreeing to move abroad with her husband and regardless of all the tribulations that she may face in so doing, the opportunities for growth and personal, social, and economic advancement are boundless.

CHAPTER II

The Choice

THE TASK OF DECIDING WHETHER TO ACCEPT an overseas assignment is never easy. There are so many factors to consider, and usually there is little real information to go on and little time in which to make the decision.

It was quite an ordinary Sunday morning—with one exception: we were about to move abroad and it felt as if we were about to jump into a void.

On Friday my husband told me that the company had offered him a job in Africa. I took the news calmly then.

It had not come as a surprise, really. For over a year my husband had been talking about how much he wanted to break into the international scene and how good it would be for his career if he did.

I was a bit dazed throughout the weekend; and now—as I stood washing the breakfast dishes, watching my small children play in the yard, and listening to my husband cheer on his favorite football team—I began to cry. I would be leaving so much of my family and all of my friends behind.

How could we know, how could we decide what was best for us? Why should we leave?

There are questions and more questions. Why should you leave? Will the transfer really benefit the employee's career? What about the other members of the family? Are there legitimate reasons for refusing an overseas post? What will happen to the employee's career if he or she refuses the transfer? If, on the other hand, you decide to accept, what then?

We have no pat answers for you. We can, however, share the knowledge we gained by being expatriates ourselves. You may not be cut out for it. That is a question that you have to answer. Whether a refusal will hurt the employee's career depends on the employee and the company. Needless to say, it is far better to be honest and to say "no" if a move will really be detrimental to you and your family. To say "yes" against your better judgment and find out later that you made the wrong decision will cost you, your family, and your company much anguish and money. *But how can you know if the decision to move is right for you before you've made it?*

You have some hard thinking to do. We will try to give you as much helpful information as possible—information that we certainly could have used ourselves when we were faced with the question. *Be honest with yourself, and make sure you consider all of your options* before you make your decision. Also—and we cannot stress this point too much—*make sure that everyone in the family has a chance to voice his or her opinion about the move, because everyone in the family is going to have to live with the decision.* A unilateral decision to accept or reject an overseas post, without the understanding and agreement of the other family members, does not make for a solid foundation to support the family when the consequences of that decision come to pass. There may be good reason to weigh some family members' opinions more than others, but everyone in the family should have a say. You are all going to have to pull together, wherever you live.

What Are the Factors?

The various factors you must evaluate are to a great extent individual. There are, however, standard questions to be asked and answered by anyone confronted with the decision of accepting an overseas assignment or not. The answers to these questions should give you a very strong indication as to whether the move will be right for you and your family.

—Where is the job? What do you know about the host country? What don't you know?

—How long will the assignment last: months, years, indefinitely?

—What makes you think that you are or are not suited to live and work overseas? What are you looking forward to? What are you afraid of? What are your expectations?

—What about the other members of the family? Are they suited to living overseas? What are their special needs? What are they looking forward to? What are they afraid of? What are their expectations?

—Is your family generally flexible and adaptable?

—Will living overseas be a severe hardship—emotional or physical—on any family member? Is there any family member who should not move?

—What is the job? Is it a promotion? Is it a good career move?

—Will the job make the spouse-employee more visible to his superiors? Will the job provide greater challenges and responsibilities? Will the spouse-employee be in close contact with the home office, or is the job actually an outposting?

—Will taking the job mean more money and a better standard of living?

—What are the legal implications of an overseas move?

—What effect will the overseas posting have on your taxes and net income?

—What potential does the job have? What kind of job can the spouse-employee expect to be offered next?

—What kinds of emotional and financial sacrifices will the other members of the family have to make in order to effect the move? Will you have to curtail your career? What will the children have to sacrifice?

—How will the children's education be affected?

—What are the alternatives to accepting the move?

These questions may seem endless, especially as each one leads to others. There is some danger in having too much information, because you can become overloaded and confused. Everyone will have a different point of view—you, your spouse, your children, your friends and family, the company—and each one may be at odds with the others.

Certainly the company wants you to move; otherwise your husband would not have been offered the position. Therefore, the company is likely to be receptive to at least considering suggestions that would satisfy your needs in order to satisfy its own. It is a matter of figuring out what your needs and goals are and how they balance with those of your spouse, the other members of your family, and the company. In reviewing the answers given in our survey, we were able to compile the following suggestions as to how to make the decision process easier.

Make Lists

Using the questions noted above and others that you can think of, you and your spouse should independently *make lists of the pros and cons* of the anticipated move and of alternatives that you may have (accepting the transfer, refusing, having the family stay behind while the employee moves, having some but not all family members move).

Set Time Limits

The company will probably have given you a limited period in which to make your decision. You have a great deal of work to do within this period. Set a time limit for compiling your lists, investigating options, and gathering facts. Do not give yourself too much time, however, as this will give you and your spouse a tempting opportunity to procrastinate. This may only lead to a last-minute and ill-thought-out decision. Our feeling is that seven to fourteen days is a sufficient amount of time to come to the decision.

Organize Your Information

Categorize the information that you gather and choose a system that will allow you to assign values to each of the pros and cons, such as a number system that involves pluses and minuses. This will help you to put your feelings, the facts, and your expectations into proper perspective. *Do not undervalue your feelings simply because they are intangible.* They are just as real and important as the facts because your feelings affect your attitude, and in making your decisions your attitude is essential for positive experiences.

Compare

Compare your lists with those of your spouse, and talk about the benefits, costs, and rewards of each alternative. Identify your individual priorities and talk about how each of you wants to achieve your goals. *Be honest.* Look at the tradeoffs that each of you will have to make if you accept the assignment, and talk about which trade-offs are worth this move.

There are good reasons for refusing a transfer altogether or for opting to have some of the family stay behind. Your children may be too young to withstand the rigors of a hardship posting. Or they may be teenagers, ready to finish their high school educations and therefore unwilling to move. Another situation that could cause a real dilemma is that of the two-career couple: what if you are at a critical stage in your own career? Perhaps a temporary separation is the answer, whereby the spouse-employee makes the move and you stay behind. Perhaps the spouse-employee's company will be willing to help you make a comparable transfer from one position to another so that neither spouse's career will be jeopardized by the move. There are a lot of options if you think creatively.

Corporations are not mind readers. There are reasons for refusing to make a move that are purely personal and quite legitimate, but the company has to be made aware of them. You will probably find that the corporation will be willing to "go the extra mile" for you if there are extenuating personal circumstances that make the transfer a major hardship for you. After all, the company needs and wants the spouse-employee to take the job and is likely to be willing to respond to your needs.

My husband was offered a very exciting opportunity that involved a move to Europe and a great leap for his career. The children and I were really looking forward to the move.

Then the bomb dropped: my doctor told me I had cancer. We thought we couldn't move, and my husband had to tell the company that he could not accept the new position.

But, you know, the company was wonderful! They agreed to pay for all air transportation, phone consultations, and baby-sitting costs when I would have to be away from the children.

We made the move, and I'm more than just happy to tell you that my cancer was "cured." What's more: living overseas has been everything we hoped it would be.

Whatever your situation—whether you are a one- or two-career couple, and whether you have children or not—the basic rules for making the best decision are:

1. Be open and honest with yourself and with your spouse about what you really want and need.

2. Be ready to listen to your spouse and give "equal consideration" to what he or she really wants and needs.

3. If you have children, give them a chance to have their say as well, even if you choose not to give them a full vote in the decision. You need their understanding and agreement and you will be far more likely to get it if they feel that they have been part of the decision-making process.

4. Don't regard the spouse-employee's company as a ruling tyrant. The company needs the spouse-employee's skills. It needs to know what will make the spouse-employee (and therefore his or her family) happy with the transfer. So speak up. Chances are the company will at least meet you halfway. Whatever you do, don't accept the

transfer because you feel that you have absolutely no other alternative. To move unwillingly usually results in a bad overseas experience and early termination, which will certainly not benefit you or the company. *You do have other alternatives.*

Temporary Separation

This is not an attractive alternative, but it happens all the time and may, in fact, be the most appropriate alternative for you at the moment. Actually, most expatriate families experience periods of temporary separation while they are preparing to move: usually the spouse-employee is sent to the new post immediately while the rest of the family packs and prepares to move. For some families this situation occurs so often that it becomes a matter of routine. One wife jokingly remarked that her husband traveled so much that she was tempted to redecorate their bedroom to look like a hotel room so that he would feel "at home" on his return.

Separation from one's family is never easy, but with foresight, planning, and some cooperation from the company the strain can be minimized. In those cases when the spouse-employee and his family decide that the spouse-employee should be the only person to make the move, the company may respond by agreeing to regular and often liberal home leaves.

In cases where the family includes older children who would not benefit from the move, there are temporary separation options: the children can live with relatives, the families of school friends, or they can go to boarding schools in the States. In such cases, you may be able to negotiate summer home leaves and travel benefits for the child to join the family in the host country for major holidays.

You and your spouse and children are the only ones who can figure out what will be best for you. The company can help to design a plan that will be mutually acceptable to all. You just have to make sure that you are honest with yourselves and with the company, and you have to make sure that you are all aware of what is at stake and the compromises to be made.

Tough issues will arise when you consider moving—they always do. We try here to describe what those issues are likely to be and what solutions may be appropriate. *There are always solutions.* Our suggestions and questions should be just the beginning. They are meant to trigger your thoughts. Be reasonable, be flexible, be creative, be positive in your outlook, and the answers should materialize.

PART TWO

CHAPTER III

Educating Your Children Overseas

THE EDUCATION OF CHILDREN IS A MAJOR CONCERN to parents living overseas. Typical worries include the quality of education, the dedication of overseas teachers to their profession, the quality of school facilities, the benefits of a bilingual/multilingual education, and the effect of an overseas education on college entrance.

In most cases the fear that a child will not receive an adequate education is misplaced. There are many alternative forms of education to consider and evaluate. The greatest dilemma results from a transfer to an area where there is no school. Even this can be overcome.

One of the most common misconceptions is thinking that schooling is automatically better in the States than abroad. To put your mind at ease, remember that peer pressure works as well overseas as at home. Given that students frequently do not view studying as the "in" thing to do, there may be distinct advantages for your child overseas. Most expatriate students are enrolled in private schools—many of which have limited enrollment and are in a position to refuse admission to students who do not perform. Consequently, expatriate students tend to realize quickly that they had better study or else. There is also the isolation factor. Children abroad do not have as much freedom to move about or work, nor are they as exposed to countless hours of television. Hence, many children tend to concentrate more on their studies. An additional factor is that, in all probability, your child will find the new school to be one where the majority of parents are college educated and his or her classmates are college bound. Peer group pressure in this environment encourages good study habits and the desire to strive for better grades.

Do not expect your child's new educational system to be an exact replica of the U.S. system. It may differ in many ways and, in fact, often does. Keep in mind that there are pluses and minuses in all situations and what your child might lose in one area he or she may gain in another.

The child who lives overseas will have many advantages over the child who never leaves the United States. The expatriate child will have travel opportunities beyond the reach of the average American and will have the opportunity, in a natural setting, to learn the ways of other people and to speak with them in their language. As the child copes with the new environment, he or she will gain a maturity, independence, and self-confidence not often found in stateside children of the same age.

Let Your Child Participate in the Decision

The academic issue is not a parent's only concern. For some children, switching schools can be a traumatic experience. Your child's feelings must be considered. If your child has just won a coveted position on the student council, is a star athlete, or captain of the cheerleaders, you can expect resistance to a move. This is only natural. To lessen the trauma, make sure your child has a voice in all the decisions that affect him or her, including education.

It would certainly be helpful if parents were endowed with clairvoyance or had a crystal ball to assure themselves that moving abroad would not cause problems for their offspring. But in the absence of such powers, parents must rely on the expertise of educators, psychologists, guidance counselors, and personnel directors. Most of all, though, parents must rely on the personal experiences of the children themselves:

> Our daughter had attended a Montessori system ever since she entered school, and so we chose not to send her to the two-thousand-student ASOS school. We felt the noise and lack of discipline would be more than she could cope with. Boy, were we wrong.
>
> We sent her to a private school with a small student body, but she was unhappy and became a discipline problem. For two years we tried everything to overcome the situation, while she kept begging us to send her to the American school. We finally relented and, once she settled down, we discovered the whole problem had been her lack of friends. Most of the other children her age, who spoke her language, went to the American school.
>
> Since that episode we've always consulted our daughter when making any decisions about her education.

What Are the Educational Opportunities?

Options for schooling overseas include: ASOS (American-Sponsored Overseas Schools); U.S. Department of Defense Overseas Dependent Schools; private preparatory schools; company schools (schools set up and run by a corporation for employees' children); mission schools; correspondence schools; co-op tutoring programs; public and private host country schools; and schools sponsored by other countries. If none of these appeal to you and your child, you may even start your own school. Some people have! Alternatively, you could have your child remain at school in the States, living with friends or relatives, or enrolled in a boarding school.

Make sure, when you decide with your child on a school, that you are satisfied with its accreditation. Your child's status in his or her next school may depend on this. Occasionally good students are required to repeat a year because their prior school was not properly accredited. Many schools, including most ASOS schools, are accredited by U.S. accreditation associations and/or by the host country's department of education.

To find out more about school systems overseas, you may wish to obtain information from one or more of the following sources:

"Overseas American-Sponsored Elementary and
    Secondary Schools Assisted by the U.S. Department
    of State"
Office of Overseas Schools (ASOS)
Room 234, SA-6
U.S. Department of State
Washington, DC 20520
Telephone: (703) 875-7800

Schools Abroad of Interest to Americans (1988–89)

Porter Sargent Publishers, Inc.
11 Beacon Street
Boston, MA 02108

The Private School Handbook
Porter Sargent Publishers, Inc.
11 Beacon Street
Boston, MA 02108

Peterson's Independent Secondary Schools 1990–91
Peterson's Guides
P. O. Box 2123
Princeton, NJ 08543-2123

Private Independent Schools
Bunting and Lyon
238 N. Main Street
Wallingford, CT 06492

The American-Sponsored Overseas School System

ASOS schools are probably the most popular alternative for expatriate children. The ASOS system has two major goals: to educate children according to stateside educational practices, and to promote intercultural understanding. Schools in the ASOS system are generally nonprofit and nonsectarian. This system typically offers education from the elementary through the secondary levels and employs mostly U.S. or U.S.-trained teachers, supervisors, and administrators who follow U.S. or binational curriculum guidelines.

The student bodies of ASOS schools are composed of host-country children, third-country children, U.S. government dependents, children of private U.S. citizens who are permanent residents in the host country, and children of private U.S. citizens who work for U.S. corporations.

ASOS schools are primarily funded by tuition, Office of Overseas Schools grants, and local business and government contributions. A common misconception is to believe that, since the U.S. government helps to support ASOS schools, all are identical in terms of facilities, staff, curriculum, and admissions standards. They are not. Schools, including those in the ASOS system, can differ markedly. Find out all you can about the origin, goals, facilities, and accreditation of each school you consider.

United States Department of Defense Overseas Dependent Schools

This is the largest U.S.-sponsored overseas school system. Each military branch runs its own subsystem. The drawback for private sector families is that these schools are normally restricted to dependents of U.S. military personnel. However, if no other type of schooling is available, write to the U.S. Department of Defense to explain your plight: U.S. Department of Defense, Office of Dependent Schools, Hoffman Building #1, Room 152, 2461 Eisenhower Avenue, Alexandria, VA 22331. Telephone: (703) 325-0660.

Mission Schools

If you have a direct working or personal relationship with the mission or the school itself, mission schools may be an option for your child. Many such schools have been organized for the benefit of the local citizens and the children of the mission staff. As such they are not usually open to children of other U.S. citizens.

Private Schools

There are many different types of private schools catering to different needs. For a fee, educational counselors and organizations are available to assist in making the appropriate selection, getting your child accepted, and advising on available scholarships. If you are in a hurry to select a school or are unfamiliar with the process, it could be beneficial to use such professional services.

Correspondence Schools

Correspondence courses for your child may be arranged through your hometown school system, a college, university, or a professional correspondence school. Be aware, though, that education by correspondence is difficult and sometimes frustrating, especially for a teenager. Both parents and students taking correspondence courses must be persistent, well motivated, and self-disciplined.

One of the most popular correspondence schools for children overseas is the Calvert School, which was founded in 1897. The program covers kindergarten through eighth grade. No previous teaching experience is necessary to use the Calvert system. You will be provided with step-by-step instructions and daily lesson plans. Tuition covers instruction manuals, books, supplies, placement tests, and guidance by a professional teacher. The Calvert program is approved by the Department of Education of the State of Maryland. For further information, contact: Calvert School, 105 Tuscany Road, Baltimore, MD 21210. Telephone: (301) 243-6030.

For information concerning accredited high school correspondence programs, contact:

Independent Study High School
University of Nebraska, Lincoln
269 NCCE
Lincoln, NB 68583-0900
Telephone: (402) 472-1926

High School Correspondence Course, U.C. Extension

223 Fulton Street
Berkeley, CA 94720
Telephone: (415) 642-4124

Host Country Schools

Some parents send their children to a local host country school, with both children and parents pleasantly pleased with the results. This type of school can be especially beneficial for children who already speak the language or who expect to be residing in the country for an extended period of time.

Few parents elect this option, however, for a number of reasons. First, there is a concern that their children will have difficulties educationally, as well as socially, because of their inability to speak the local language. This often results in the children feeling like "outsiders." Another drawback is that an expatriate child may encounter an entirely different educational philosophy and methodology from that of his or her home school system. Also, behavioral traditions observed by students and teachers in the host country may run counter to those of the child's upbringing.

Occasionally, parents who plan to live in the host country indefinitely may elect to educate their children in host country schools, feeling that total immersion in the culture, as well as accelerated language development, outweighs other drawbacks.

Schools Sponsored by Other Countries

Americans overseas are not the only ones concerned that their children will not receive an education equivalent to that which is available at home. For this reason you may find German, French, British, or Japanese schools in your new locale. You may opt to enroll your child in one of these schools.

An important factor to keep in mind is how such a variety of changes may affect your child. He or she may have to confront learning two languages and two new cultures. This decision will depend for the most part on the maturity, motivation, and educational background of your particular child.

Questions to Ask and Answer Before Choosing an Overseas School

In this section we list a number of questions that you should ask about the schools and programs you are considering for your child. If you do not receive all the answers or the type of answers you require, go elsewhere and dig. Fellow church members, other newcomers, or co-workers are wonderful information sources. Remember, too, that students who are already enrolled in the schools you are looking at are very good sources of information.

Enrollment

—Will your children be automatically accepted or must they pass admissions tests and/or fill out application forms?

—Are there any quotas for students of particular nationalities?

—How large are the classes?

—What is the size of the student body?

—What is the composition of the student body?

—Are children who lack proficiency in the English language accepted?

—What about children who lack proficiency in the host country language?

—What documents are needed for official enrollment?

Board Members/Administrators/Staff

—What are the general qualifications of each group?

—Has there been a continuity of leadership?

—Is there a staff psychologist or counselor?
—Is there a librarian?
—Who are the auxiliary staff members?
—How many staff members are there per pupil?
—Is there an effective PTA?
—Who are the members of the school board?
—How are the members of the school board chosen?

Curriculum

—Is the curriculum college preparatory and/or vocational?
—Is it a bilingual program? If so, of what type?
—Are there any cultural or governmental constraints?
—Does the curriculum meet the needs of short-term, monolingual students?
—Is there a single-track curriculum?
—Does the curriculum allow for re-entry into U.S. school systems and/or host country higher education systems?
—What provisions are made for the highly gifted child?
—What provisions are made for the child with a learning disability?
—What extracurricular activities does the school provide?
—Does the school provide a summer program?

Facilities

—What exactly are the school's facilities?
—Is there a library, a gymnasium, an audiovisual department, an art studio, a music department, a science lab, a computer lab?
—Is there a bus service?
—Is there a meal service?
—Are there medical services?

School Calendar
—Does the school year correspond to the U.S. school year or your needs?
—What holidays are observed?
—How many hours per day and how many days per week will your child be in school?

Finances
—Are the finances of the school sufficient to provide an adequate curriculum?
—Who funds the school?
—What are the tuition fees?
—Are there scholarships available?
—What extra charges are there (music, dance, summer school, social events, tutoring)?
—Does the school participate in college scholarship programs?

Philosophy
—By whom is the school accredited?
—What is the school's attitude toward monolingualism? Bilingualism?
—Is the school's philosophy based on long-term or short-term participation by students?
—What is the behavior code of the school?
—What is the school's dress code?
—What is the school's attitude toward homework?

Will Your Children Be Accepted by the Schools of Their Choice?

Unfortunately, there are no guarantees for acceptance. Many schools have quotas for students of particular nationalities. There may also be proficiency tests to be passed or behavioral standards to be met. Contact the schools you are considering as early as possible and be sure to visit each on your first trip to the host country.

Are Expatriate Children Readily Accepted into U.S. School Systems When They Return?

In general, returning students (especially those who transfer from an American school system) are as readily accepted into a U.S. school as they would be if they were transferring from another U.S. neighborhood. Overseas schools are usually very efficient about forwarding transcripts and records.

Expatriate parents often find their children are stronger in languages, literature, history, geography, and current events than their stateside peers. Conversely, expatriate children may lack certain innovations in math, science, and sports training. It will depend on the individual school and its system of education and teachers.

A frequent experience following a transfer back to the States was related by one parent:

When my children transferred from an overseas school to a public school in the States, I was afraid that they wouldn't be accepted by their peers. To my surprise and relief, not only were they accepted, they were actually looked up to and sought after. They were elected to class offices and well respected for their special knowledge and insights. My youngest child found school much easier in the United States. "It's in the same language all day!" he exclaimed gleefully.

Will Your Children Have Difficulty Getting into College?

There is probably little need for the parent of a student enrolled in an ASOS school or another American overseas school to worry. College counselors are available at most schools, and college entrance examinations are given just as they are in the States.

In fact, universities look favorably on students with areas of special expertise or experience. Students in American Overseas Secondary Schools, and most of the other types of private schools, study the host country language and have the advantage of a natural language lab right in their backyards. Students are also encouraged to take additional languages as electives. Many do, given the atmosphere of cross-cultural communication. As a result, the language achievement scores of expatriate students tend to be quite high.

If your child is approaching college age, make the proper arrangements for all examinations and collect college catalogues well in advance, as well as all necessary documents and forms. You should also arrange for visits to the colleges and universities. Or, take advantage of the college-sponsored summer programs for high school juniors, which often include interviews and campus tours of more than just the sponsoring colleges.

Check to see that your child's records are complete, especially if he or she has been to several schools. For each school attended, you should include a description of the school, courses taken, and the marking system. Since it has been an advantage for your child to have lived overseas, send along a detailed description of overseas travel, work, and volunteer experiences.

If your child is not in an American overseas school you may have more legwork to do but do not despair. If you've been careful all along to provide the best possible education—in the school, at home, and in extracurricular and summer activities—and if your child really wants to go to college, the extra effort will pay off. For further information, write to:

College Entrance Examination Board
Department R21, College Board Publications
Box 886
New York, NY 10101-0886
Telephone: (212) 713-8165

Ask for the "College Handbook, Foreign Student Supplement, 1991." This booklet and the CEEB staff will be able to assist you.

Remember, there are deadlines for achievement and aptitude tests, submission of applications, and fee payments. It's best to plan well ahead as you are responsible for making sure that all deadlines are met. If all of this seems overwhelming, you may want to enlist the aid of a private counselor, who will guide you through this process.

What Are the Effects of a Bilingual Education?

Many parents fear that their children will suffer if they are forced to pursue their educational careers in more than one language. Whether this is a valid concern, the fact that it is an attitude held by many is a reality. However, based on the hundreds of studies that have been made of children's language acquisition processes and the effect of bilingualism on intelligence tests, it is apparent that bilingual children's verbal skills tend to be superior. Experience suggests that parents need not worry. Language difficulties diminish rapidly under the guidance of good teachers and other significant influences, such as progress, peers, and attitude. In addition, children whose parents speak English at home will usually be English-dominant, even if they live overseas all their lives. In fact, their English will probably be freer from slang and regionalisms than that of their U.S. counterparts.

To provide for a smoother transition from a monolingual to a bilingual setting, many overseas schools offer special language classes for new arrivals. Students are given individual instruction in the new language to prepare them for regular programs.

It is usually to the student's benefit to move into the regular bilingual class as soon as possible. However, parents do have the authority to veto such a move if they feel it would be detrimental to the child's adjustment.

Although my son seemed to have a natural affinity for languages, I requested that he not be transferred to the regular bilingual program despite the fact his teacher felt he was ready to do so after only two months in the special language class. My reason was simple: his social adjustment was as important as his academic progress. He had changed schools several times and had just made friends with a fine boy in his special language class. To uproot him and force him to face another sea of unknown faces seemed almost cruel. Instead, he was allowed to finish the school year in the special class and to begin the regular program the following fall.

Children in bilingual classes usually progress so quickly that they leave older family members far behind in second language skills. Often this expertise gives children more responsibility and self-esteem within their families. Their ability to speak the local language makes them an important contributor to the family and can foster maturity.

What Special Problems Can Your Child Encounter?

The typical overseas school is in a constant state of change. One would hope that education would be an element of stability for the child; but, unfortunately, it seldom is. Most overseas schools are subject to a high turnover of students, parents, teachers, administrators, school boards, and general supporters. Hence, overseas schools tend to lack two basic components that most stateside schools take for granted: continuity and tradition.

If you determine to keep your children in one "style" of education you will establish a basic continuity; otherwise you will need to be flexible. For instance, if you've just moved from Germany to Mexico and the new school does not have German language classes, you and your child will have a number of options: start from square one with Spanish language classes; arrange for a German language tutor whose lessons will be accepted for credit by the school; or both. This can happen in math and science as well. At worst, your child could be required to repeat a semester or carry a heavier academic load.

Costs

Education is often more costly abroad than in the States. Greater expenses are incurred because much of the staff is imported; therefore, not only must salary, pension, and health care be covered, but housing and relocation costs also become a factor. There are additional costs involved in the transportation of books, meals, instructional supplies, and equipment. Plus there is the cost of busing students to and from the school, as it is unlikely that all the students live near the school. Most schools depend on revenue from tuition, private industry donations, and government grants. Many expatriate parents have been known to become involved in raising funds to supplement limited budgets.

Curriculum

The curriculum is another area to investigate. What is it?

— Is the curriculum strictly college preparatory or are vocational opportunities available?
— Does the curriculum coincide with the curriculum back home?
— What language will be used?
— What extracurricular activities are there—debate club, science club, choir?
— What type of athletics program is there?

The answers to these questions will require you and your child to make a number of personal decisions when selecting an overseas school.

As one of our interviewees explained,

I had three children of school age when we moved to Spain. Two of my children adjusted beautifully to the American school. The program was identical to that of our home state, and so they had little trouble adapting. But our other child, a daughter, was miserable beyond words. We really didn't know what to do, nor could we pinpoint the specific problem.

Eventually, we decided to pull her out of the American school and place her in a local school. The curriculum was oriented, of course, to Spanish speakers. But our company was marvelous and provided a daily tutor for her. At it turned out, she became totally bilingual and received outstanding marks. The decision we made was right. It wouldn't necessarily have been for the other two.

Certain schools may choose to follow a curriculum based on long-term participation, especially for language development. For the family who is extremely mobile and changes schools on a yearly or biyearly basis, such a philosophy is likely to cause problems. While tutors can help to bring your child up to speed, many parents dislike the need for the child to spend the extra time away from the family and regular school activities.

Then there are schools which try to satisfy all members of the student body and at least two different governments' educational policies. Such schools opt to have students spend half of the day following a curriculum designed for re-entry into the home-country school system and the other half of the day following a curriculum designed for entry into a higher educational facility in the host country. Usually, when the student reaches eighth or ninth grade he or she must choose the ultimate curriculum that will be followed.

Remember, the curriculum abroad does not have to be the same as that in the States. There should be a basic continuity in core courses, but otherwise each school should take advantage of its local resources as to history, language, culture, and sports. For instance, skiing is a gym class in Canada; marksmanship, in Israel; and swimming, in Mexico. Museums and art galleries, theater, and tours of historic sights are all part of education in Europe. Visiting other foreign countries is often a large part of the social studies/language curriculum overseas. This type of exposure more than makes up for the lack of a large, modern building or a huge library.

Special Children

A child with learning disabilities or special talents may find that his or her needs will not be met in all overseas locations. Special needs frequently demand extra attention, wherever you are living. If you cannot find an appropriate school in your new host country for your special child, a viable alternative may be to use a correspondence school program or a cooperative tutoring program.

Facilities

Is the school plant itself a factor in the education your child receives? Opinions vary considerably on this point. We have gone from row after row of neatly aligned chairs, with chalk and chalkboard being the teacher's only means of instruction, to a variety of chair and desk formations, with a multitude of bulletin boards and countless audiovisual instructional aids. What you find overseas runs the gamut. Some schools have huge physical plants, with libraries for various age groups, media centers, tennis courts, swimming pools, and gymnasiums. Other schools are based on the "one-room schoolhouse" concept. Many parents prefer one type of atmosphere to another. But if the choice is limited, don't let it upset you. Children are amazingly flexible and usually adapt to new situations quite easily.

Our children have experienced sleek modern plants, mediocre plants, and now an old convent, complete with thatched-roof dormitories and stables converted to classrooms. There is no gym yet (fundraising has begun) and the auditorium is an old chapel. None of this has negatively influenced the children. The attitude and quality of the staff—and their ingenuity, resources, and abilities—have provided the impact.

Parents, in my opinion, are more impressed by school plants. Kids don't care how big the library or auditorium seats are. The atmosphere for learning is provided by the teacher—ugly, old bare walls can be just as educationally stimulating as new ones if a teacher wishes to make them so. It's not the four walls; it's what the teacher does within them that counts.

The School Calendar

Overseas school calendars may or may not coincide with the States as to days of instruction, holidays, or vacations. Some schools, cognizant of expatriates' desires to return to the U.S. during the summer or Christmas holidays, have adjusted their schedules accordingly and offer six-week vacations during those times. In some countries, especially where local nationals attend the school, schools may coordinate their schedules with local holidays. In other countries, where weather is an important factor or where children are still needed to help bring in the crops, the school calendars are adapted accordingly.

Class Size

As in the United States, there are cases where class enrollment exceeds the recommended limit of 15–24 pupils per classroom because of limited facilities. Such crowding leads many parents to wonder if their children are receiving sufficient individual attention. Again, this really depends on the teachers. Some teachers actually find large classes easier to handle. The key consideration here is the teacher to whom your child has been assigned. One way to alleviate this is to offer your services as a teacher's aid. Another is to volunteer as a fund raiser to secure the necessary funding for a salaried assistant.

The Staff

No one statement can cover the quality of the staff in every school. In some cases you may find that the quality of the overseas teaching is superior to that found in the States. Unfortunately, in some cases, there are individuals who have been hired for teaching positions when they are not qualified. Occasionally, teachers who are not local nationals cannot get working papers, and untrained local nationals may be hired because they speak the languages of the students. *This does not happen in all schools,* but it happens often enough that, as a parent, you should be aware of it.

If there is an American school where you are located, the staff will almost certainly be composed of certified professionals or student teachers who are working toward their stateside certification. They may have been hired originally because they hold a bachelor of arts degree (whether or not it is in the field of their present position), but most American schools require their teachers to receive stateside credentials in order to continue their employment.

You may find that teachers in school systems abroad range from the totally untrained to highly dedicated professionals. Whether these individuals will be devoted to the job and your child will be just as much a matter of the individual as it is for any teacher in the U.S. *There are good teachers and bad teachers everywhere.*

Extracurricular Activities

Generally speaking, extracurricular activities for children outside the United States need parental support and involvement. If you have a special talent—photography, tennis, art, whatever—offer your services. Rarely do you have to be a trained instructor. Get somebody to assist you, but don't hold back. You will find that you will be personally rewarded many times over. You will be filling your time constructively as well as sparking an interest for a child in something that he or she may never have otherwise known about. On top of this, you just might be the motivating force behind a child beginning to succeed academically and socially. Children, just as adults, need mentors. Many children have gone on from their initial confidence-building extracurricular activities to become experts in their outside interests. Share your talents with a child and you'll never regret it.

Summer Programs

Some school systems offer extensive summer programs which other school systems do not. Check with your schools to find out what summer programs are available locally and in other countries. Once again, this is an area in which you can be very active. You can volunteer to help set up and administer a program. You can offer your services as a teacher. You can join with other parents to devise your own summer program.

Also, in many countries, students can obtain an identity card which entitles them to discounted or free admission to museums, theaters, concerts, youth hostels, restaurants, and travel tours. For information on these cards and their function, check with your school.

What Educational Supplies Should You Carry When You Move to the Host Country?

Of course, what you decide to bring will depend on your destination. If you are headed for a very primitive area of the world you should probably bring everything— pencils, paper, books, and the like. If you are to reside in a large metropolitan city with a U.S.-style school system, everything is likely to be supplied through the school.

Generally speaking, it is wise to pack a dictionary and thesaurus in your hand luggage, as well as left-handed supplies for your left-handers. If you plan to bring a personal computer, make sure it meets your host country's electronic specifications.

From the Students' Point of View

To help answer some of the questions which probably come to mind concerning your child's education abroad, we went directly to the "experts"—the children. The respondents ranged in age from six to nineteen and represented a wide variety of nationalities. All of the students spoke at least two languages. A few of the students had moved as many as fourteen times and were well prepared to discuss various aspects of relocation, such as how it affected their schooling and their family relationships. What follows is a listing of our questions and a cross-section of the students' most common responses.

How Does Moving Affect Your Schooling?

I find no difference in schooling. The only thing that it may affect is making friends.

*   *   *

For me, school has been easier. I have many friends and they are all very nice. I have almost the same texts and courses, and all my teachers are good.

* * *

Losing friends, not understanding teachers and their methods, or what they expect from you, plus new subjects—one has to learn to adjust to all this.

* * *

Courses, the same—but I do better in school. Sports are basically the same, but it's easier to be a "star" in Mexico than in the U.S.A. Also, I have closer friends in Mexico.

* * *

In my other school they did not teach me much, so it is very difficult for me and I am repeating a year.

* * *

I think it makes you feel closer to new friends and teachers. It's hard to become active in sports and clubs, and sometimes you end up taking courses you have already taken.

* * *

You have fewer friends—but closer ones.

* * *

I've had to repeat courses at the high school level and my brother has had to repeat courses at the college level because of our new schools' requirements and the transit problems of transcripts. I miss my old modern dance and yoga classes. Places of officership have never opened to me in clubs as I never remained in one place long enough to attain seniority.

*   *   *

There is less competition here, fewer clubs and organizations. Everything is on a smaller scale. You have a chance to be noticed and to excel.

What Are the Greatest Benefits Derived from Your Moves?

International viewpoint, many different friends, additional languages, cultural experiences, opportunity to travel.

*   *   *

Gained great knowledge about world cultures, had incredible experiences. Worth it!

*   *   *

Opens your mind to new ideas, regained individuality, and expanded knowledge of culture.

*   *   *

The family grows closer together. You appreciate being with your relatives more.

*   *   *

A chance to learn something new every day.

*   *   *

Deeper friendships.

*   *   *

Adventure.

*   *   *

You meet new people from all over the States and all over the world.

*   *   *

A chance to start over again.

*   *   *

They provided great high school and college entrance essay topics.

*   *   *

Caused me to think globally and consider an international career.

What Are the Greatest Difficulties Caused by Moving?

Leaving friends, being uprooted from schools. Also disorganization, fatigue, nostalgia.

*   *   *

Packing, finding a house, living in a hotel forever.

*   *   *

Setting up the house.

*   *   *

Facing stereotyping by other nationalities.

*   *   *

Loneliness.

*   *   *

Waiting for your furniture.

*   *   *

We've always lost household items.

*   *   *

Missing your best friend.

*   *   *

Fights among the family because of tensions caused by adjusting to different places.

Has Moving Affected the Way Your Family Gets Along? If Yes, in What Way?

No, we get along the same.

*   *   *

We've learned to rely on each other more.

*   *   *

Yes: much pressure, family quarrels, low moods, crises.

*   *   *

Yes, my brother and I are really close friends. I don't think we would have been if we hadn't had to depend on each other so much.

*   *   *

It's made us a lot closer than most American families.

CHAPTER IV

Career Women
Abroad

ACCORDING TO EVERY STUDY OF EXPATRIATES, including
our own, one of the greatest threats to a successful
overseas assignment is the unhappiness of the employee's
spouse and/or children. It is rare that the corporate employee poses the problem.

In an international move, more than in any other experience, there is the likelihood that wives will experience
feelings of loss, isolation, loneliness, fear, and depression.
This is especially true after the family has moved into its
new home, the servant has been hired and trained, and
the children have started school. We found that such feelings are so closely related to feelings of boredom that it is
impossible to deal with them separately. "Be flexible and
keep busy" were two of the best bits of advice we heard
over and over again from the women we interviewed; and
our own experiences have certainly led us to the same
conclusion.

Pursuing a career is an obvious solution to being bored or lonely. However, because of the tremendous effort and concentration involved in overseeing a transnational move, expatriate wives put off looking for work until after they and their families have settled into their new environments.

In many countries, women are an accepted part of the work force, holding jobs all the way up the managerial ladder. One of our sources held middle and senior level marketing management positions with various U.S.-based multinational corporations in Brazil, Portugal, and Mexico. She said that she experienced fewer problems and less discrimination in such supposedly "macho" countries than she had expected. A major reason for this, she said, was that her U.S. business education and experience gained her automatic respect. She gave us the following example:

> One of my subordinates in Portugal was a male chauvinist par excellence. At a cocktail party, he remarked in my presence that he would never work for a woman. Shocked, I demanded to know how he could say such a thing, since he reported to me. He replied, "That's different. You're not a woman; you're an American woman. That makes you as good as any man."

In many other countries, women are definitely not an accepted part of the work force; they are looked upon as oddities, if they are allowed to work at all. Some countries even have laws prohibiting paid employment for foreign women. Our sources also have reported that, although women are not legally prohibited from working in Far Eastern countries, it is difficult to get jobs there.

Working Papers

When you and your husband are in the process of considering the overseas assignment, make sure that he and his company are aware of your wish to work. Also make sure that you look over all your husband's work documents in order to delete any reference to you as a dependent. *If you sign a document that identifies you as a dependent, it is more than likely that you will not be able to work while you are abroad.* This will be true even if you are offered a job before your move.

Because the host country has a vested interest in making sure that its own citizens are employed before foreigners are, you may find it extremely difficult to get working papers. Before you move from the States, contact the host country consulate and, although the staff may tell you that it will be impossible for you to get working papers, find out what documents must accompany your application for working papers. Then check with your husband's company, your potential employers, and international professional employment agencies to get a more realistic idea of what you may be faced with when you try to get work in the host country.

Make sure that you have certified copies of the same documents that your spouse had to have in order to get his working papers—including all university and college diplomas, college transcripts, birth and marriage certificates, and an updated resumé. Also have available letters of introduction and recommendation, preferably on company letterheads, to verify your professional reputation. As one of our sources pointed out, "The important thing to keep in mind is that if your husband was able to obtain a work visa, a committed employer will try his best to get a work visa for you." Note however, if you are able to secure a work permit, you may be restricted as to the type of work and for whom you can work. You may also need to fulfill a residence requirement, become licensed, or take additional training or a proficiency exam in your particular field. But even these requirements have not proven to be a deterrent.

Nonprofit entrepreneurial work is one way for women to work in countries whose laws prohibit paid employment for women. Another possibility is to work for U.S. embassies or military installations. There, since you may be considered to be working in the United States, you probably won't pay local taxes and you shouldn't need work visas. You may also be paid in U.S. dollars, which may not be the case if you land a job with a local or a U.S.-based company after you and your family have moved to the host country. Of course, it would be ideal to find a job and get the appropriate working papers before you move; but in most cases, there isn't the time to do so. One important caveat: You will hear from time to time about people who work without local government approval, but this is a questionable practice that could result in costly or embarrassing consequences.

Disadvantages to Working Overseas

You probably know that it usually costs more in the United States in terms of taxes when both husband and wife work; this is also true of working overseas. If you get your job before you move, you may be paid in dollars and you may, therefore, be liable for the usual U.S. taxes. If you are a local hire, however, you will probably be paid in local currency and be liable for local taxes. Your tax liability will depend upon local tax rates, which can be negligible or exorbitant. You could conceivably pay up to eighty percent of your marginal income on taxes, so consider this point carefully before committing to a job. It is also important to know whether local law allows you to file a separate return or mandates your filing jointly with your husband. This could push your incremental income into a high tax bracket. Further, as many U.S.-based firms are not accustomed to having expatriate wives work, their tax equalization policy may not allow for your income. Before accepting an overseas assignment, sit down with your husband and a tax advisor to discuss the implications of your proposed job on your family's taxes.

While it may be expensive for you to work, if you want to work you should do so. The career and psychological benefits of working will probably far outweigh the extra tax payments you are likely to have to make. None of the working expatriate women we know has regretted the decision to work.

Advantages to Working Overseas

Aside from the obvious benefits of being busy and therefore not bored, there are some important career advantages that you will receive by working overseas. Because of your U.S. education, you will probably be perceived as an especially attractive job applicant. You are likely to be given more responsibilities in a shorter period of time than you would have been given had you stayed at home. This means that your overseas work experience will allow you to progress faster in your career when you return to the States.

Many of our sources reported that, as local hires, they received different and sometimes better fringe benefits than they would have if they'd found their jobs before moving. One woman said that two of her three overseas employers allowed her the use of a company car, whereas her husband's employer did not. Local hires also often receive bonuses that expatriate employees do not—such

as Christmas and vacation bonuses and profit sharing—
because local laws may mandate the payment of such
bonuses.

Commonly Available Types of Jobs

Obviously, your skills will determine the kinds of jobs
you will hold overseas. The very fact that you speak English is a skill. As we have indicated, if you have a U.S.
business degree or business experience you will be in the
running for managerial jobs abroad; and even if you don't
have a graduate degree, your undergraduate degree will be
worth quite a lot to foreign employers. Banking jobs at
different levels are open to women all over the world. If
you have a teaching degree, you should have little trouble
finding work in an American or international school.
Even if you don't have a teaching degree, you may be able
to teach English to employees of host-country or foreign
companies, and you can certainly teach English in your
home. There are also tourist-related jobs available in most
countries—with hotels, travel agencies, and tour companies. If you are bilingual, you should be able to find
work as a translator or a secretary. And, as we indicated
earlier, there may be openings with U.S. embassies and
military installations, although preference is usually
given to dependents of U.S. government employees.

In addition, some expatriate wives have drawn on their
training and experience and written articles for professional journals at home and abroad or have given professional seminars; some have arranged to become consul-
tants to their prior company's local subsidiary; others
have convinced their employers that they would be an
ideal liaison (at no relocation expense) in a country where
the company might not be represented but have business
or potential business. One woman even convinced local

TV and radio stations of the need for an English-language program and that she could fill the need.

Many other expatriate women set up their own businesses, based on their particular talents. For instance, in Mexico, a number of American women set up a house rental referral firm that catered to the needs of the transient expatriate community. Women in a number of foreign cities have set up gourmet shops that provide homemade foods and imported hard-to-get ingredients. One group of women in Lebanon started a nonprofit store in Beirut that sold products made by small Lebanese cottage industries. Other women, who preferred to work at home, started classes in their particular areas of talent—painting, aerobics, word processing, cooking, bridge, sewing, archeology, gemology, photography, handicrafts, flower arranging, pet obedience classes, parent effectiveness training, CPR, and first aid, to name but a few.

Others have set up tax, word processing, and secretarial services in their homes; started tutorial services for children with special learning needs; set up groups to organize and plan conferences and conventions in their city; written travel guides for the area; or published photographic studies of their host country. Some women have become photographic models; others have become freelance artists, designers, decorators, therapists, and hair stylists.

You know best what your skills and needs are, and therefore, in what types of jobs you will be interested. No matter where you are posted, there are work opportunities, though you may have to look harder for them in some areas than in others. You may not find the same job as the one you held in the United States, but jobs are there. They key is to mold a desired job out of the opportunities at hand.

Other Alternatives

Many women reported that they turned to volunteer work, some to fill their time, some to keep their hand in their field. Although they received no monetary remuneration, the opportunity to work in an international environment was sufficient compensation. For some, the volunteer work provided invaluable experience and credentials, opening up future career opportunities where none had previously existed. Many women have successfully broken into exciting new careers via their international experience.

Then, too, you may not want to work, other than for your family. Many of our interviewees said that they preferred to spend their time and energies bringing up their children and/or concentrating on their own personal growth. Many of them chose to use their overseas stay as an opportunity to further their educations. Others said that the activities available to them through their local women's clubs were such that they never got bored.

The point is this: living overseas does not have to be a boring, depressing, or isolating experience. If you put your mind to it, you will discover that there is more than enough to do that will keep you occupied, growing, and happy. Discovering what types of activities will make you happy is your responsibility. You may find that, after a year or two of living abroad and doing things you never imagined you'd get the chance to do, you will be reluctant to return home to be yet another small fish in a big pond.

PART THREE

CHAPTER V

Premove
Preparations

"I've relocated more than a dozen times and, for the most part, the moves have been relatively trouble free. The first move was obviously the most difficult, as we didn't know what to expect. After that, each move became progressively easier."

WITHOUT A DOUBT, AN INTERNATIONAL MOVE is the most difficult relocation a family can make. The magnitude and variety of unknowns, uncertainties, and unique problems are incomprehensible to the novice. Most domestic moves pale by comparison. There is so much to do and, typically, so little time in which to do it. Organization, stamina, and perseverance are essential ingredients.

More than likely you will be shipping, storing, selling, or discarding everything you and your family have accumulated for years and years. Treasured possessions will be out of your control and in the hands of others. Their safe passage and ultimate reappearance, however, are very much a function of your own preparation and hard work.

When moving you need to be in control of every aspect of the move. Of the women we surveyed, the most commonly repeated words of advice were: keep a positive attitude concerning the move, look at it as an adventure, and keep your patience and sense of humor close at hand. As unfair as it may seem, much of the move is likely to be on your shoulders. Laugh and the family will laugh with you. Complain and the family will too.

Where Are You Moving?

Advance preparation is the first step on the long road to your new home. The very first question to be answered is not, "What shall I take?" but rather, "Where am I going?" You cannot preplan a move without first knowing whether you are relocating to Paris or Nigeria. You should begin your premove preparation with a comprehensive knowledge of where you are headed.

It cannot be emphasized enough that you should familiarize yourself with what's ahead in your new country: the climate, life style, culture, schools, churches, and the availability of goods and services you enjoy or consider a necessity. Never assume that once you've made one international move you know how to do them all. Every international move is totally different. Being well informed can prevent potential problems and ease your adjustment at the same time.

Gather your information from diverse sources. Scour the libraries, tourist bureaus, consulates, book stores, international clubs, airlines, orientation services, military bases, international banks, specialty import stores, other international companies, and your local school system. Enlist the aid of relatives, friends, and even friends of

friends. Everybody and anybody can be a source of information. If you hear about someone in your town who has
lived in or visited your proposed destination, call that
person or go to see him or her with a list of questions. A
phone call, even long distance, may provide candid and
thorough answers for many of your questions. It is preferable to speak to Americans who have been or are residing
in your new home country rather than to nationals of the
country who may not understand what is essential to your
particular adjustment.

One of the most valuable sources of information, and
one not to be overlooked, is the company wives' grapevine. Short of an in-home Telex machine, this is a major
source of reliable, factual, and candid information.

When making a move, it is your responsibility to gather
as much pertinent information as possible. If you've never
moved, read a book on moving, keeping in mind the fact
that an international move is far more complex than a domestic move. Ask major moving companies to send whatever literature they distribute to their clients. Read and
reread this information. Talk to anybody who has made
an overseas move. Learn from their experiences. Don't be
surprised if you hear a lot of horror stories. There are far
more good moves than bad moves, but, unfortunately, it is
the bad experiences that are remembered and talked
about.

Is a Premove Visit Useful?

The answer to this question is YES: a trip to your new
country is invaluable. It can do much to answer many of
your questions. It will put the move into perspective and
put you several steps ahead of the game. While on the
reconnaissance trip, you may even be able to find your
new home, thereby avoiding frustration and saving

money. You may learn that you'll have to store your mammoth side-by-side refrigerator while shipping one that will fit into your new kitchen. You may come to realize that light fixtures, bathroom fixtures, or even kitchen cabinets are not available in your new home country and you may have to import them or arrange to have them handmade.

This trip can be one of the busiest times of your life and one of the most productive if you are organized and know what you are doing. Get out that notepad and start making lists of what you wish to accomplish. Take a city tour, if you have the time, so that you may begin to get the feeling of your new environment. Make sure arrangements have been made for someone to accompany you on your excursions who knows the language and the lay of the land. Driving around an unknown city can be time consuming and confusing. With a map, try to determine the distances between the residential areas, shopping centers, schools, and your husband's office. You should also take a walking tour of the different areas. Browse through the various stores, checking quality, availability, and cost of products in order to determine what should be added to your list of things to bring.

Meet with other wives from your husband's company and/or other international companies to evaluate their satisfaction with living conditions. Besides looking into housing and living standards, you may also want to observe the schools and register your children for the next semester. Find out also whether your host country schools provide educational opportunities for children who are exceptional or talented. If a member of your family is handicapped in any way, are there facilities to help with care and education? Be thorough: you may find that although there are schools for the handicapped, classes may only be held in the native language.

Remember, talk to anyone and everyone. Almost everyone has some valuable information to impart to you, so always have paper and pen ready to take notes and to list the inevitable questions which will occur to you.

Questions to Ask the Company

Before embarking on a transfer abroad it is important to initiate a dialogue with the company in order to determine the benefits to which you and your family are entitled. Investigate company policies and procedures regarding the mechanics of the move. The time to make your needs known to the head office is before you move, not two or three months later.

—Will you be allowed to select your mover or will it be selected for you?

—Will the moving company be responsible for the packing, unpacking, loading, and unloading of the goods? If not, what will be the division of labor?

—How will your goods be moved: by land, air or sea?

—Will you be allowed to move oversized or non-household items (pool tables, cars, lawn and playground equipment) at company expense? Will there be a weight limit?

—What will you be allowed to store, and at whose expense?

—Will you be allowed to ship your pet? Will the company pay for the shipment and any incidental expenses?

—Will the company pay the moving fees directly or will you be reimbursed?

—Will the company reimburse or compensate you for any added burden as a result of the move (baby sitters, food, and lodging after you've begun the packing process)?

—Will you be given temporary housing and orientation assistance upon your arrival?

One last, but very important, question to ask is: "When does the company expect you to move?" Although most moving manuals and experts recommend eight to ten weeks for the moving-out process, few expatriate wives have the luxury of this amount of time. Most are told that their husband is so valuable that his services at the new post were really needed yesterday. (More than one wife has moved in as little as one day. Incredible as that may seem, it is possible.) Even though the husband may be required to relocate immediately, company policies are usually flexible when it comes to the family.

Surprisingly, of the women we surveyed, most wives agreed they would rather not have an extensive period of time to prepare for a move. Too much time can cause family members to drop out of their social circles, to become anxious over the impending move, and to procrastinate when it comes to the details of moving. Most expatriate wives felt that thirty to sixty days were sufficient to accomplish all tasks.

Taking Notes and Making Lists

As is readily apparent from the multitude of questions you have already encountered in determining where you are going, what your host country is like, and company policies with regard to the move, it is absolutely essential that you take extensive notes and develop a systematic approach to making lists.

Should you make a list? Yes! You should make dozens of lists, each covering a different subject and each meticulously organized. For example:

—What do I need to do today?
—What appointments do I have scheduled this week?
—Who needs to be notified of our departure?
—What will I ship?
—What will I air freight?
—What will I put in storage?
—What will I give away or sell?
—What needs to be disconnected, repaired, or cleaned?
—What will I carry with me?
—What do I need to do on the final day?

Being organized, having lists and schedules and sticking to them, is vital to the success of any move. Lists really save time and avoid mental lapses. The majority of women interviewed agreed that their lists were one of the most important moving tools they had. So much happens so fast and so much has to be done that it's better to commit yourself to writing lists before the move than to a rest home afterward.

There are some helpful government publications that you may want to send for:

"Tips for Americans Abroad"
Superintendent of Documents
U. S. Government Printing Office
Washington, D.C. 20402

"Americans Abroad"
Consumer Information Center
Dept. 557X
Pueblo, CO 81009

Do You Need Any Documents Other Than Your Passports?

It is important to remember that moving internationally encompasses a host of different and more complicated procedures than moving within the United States. All countries have varied requirements and regulations. Some countries require entry visas, work permits, and import permits for personal goods, plus page upon page of forms for permission to reside in that country. In figuring out your timing, allow for numerous trips to consulates and government offices and endless hours spent in endless lines. Be sure that all your papers are in order *before* you set off on your move. Find out what documents will be required of you. This type of information should be provided by your company; if not, check with the closest consular office of your future host country as well as your moving company.

It would be a good idea to acquire a passport for each member of your family. Even small infants should have their own passports. If a mother and her children share a passport, one cannot exit the country if the other is traveling. You will appreciate having arranged for separate passports if you are out of your host country and a need arises for your child or children to travel as well.

Depending on the country you will be residing in, it may be necessary for you to have an *original*, notarized copy of each family member's birth certificate or affidavit of birth. The same may hold true for your marriage license, adoption and child custody documents, statements of nationality and religious affiliation, and all educational degrees that you have received.

To avoid delays and losses, vital documents such as the following should be *hand carried, not packed in a suitcase:* passports and visas; birth certificates, marriage and drivers' licenses, school and adoption records; medical files; moving receipts; maps; permission letter from your husband or host country form for travel with the children but without your husband; personal phone books; confirmation letters for travel accommodations; checks/bank drafts; and personal legal papers.

What About Your Legal Affairs?

Before you depart from the United States it is imperative that you put your legal affairs in order. Laws vary from state to state and country to country. It is vital that you investigate how residing abroad might alter the conditions of your will, death and inheritance taxes, the legal guardianship of your children, the citizenship of your children, powers of attorney for you and your spouse, insurance policies, taxes, and normal liabilities pertaining to your personal property. If you are going to be living in an area where communications are not speedy, you may want to consider giving your powers of attorney to someone who will supervise your investments and personal matters at home.

Investigate the laws of your new country as well. Paperwork and red tape are a fact of international life. It is important that you also be familiar with host country laws concerning death, inheritance taxes, income taxes, residence permits, work permits, car ownership, household help, contracts, leases, insurance, and contraband items. Don't be caught violating a law because of ignorance. Take the time to explore your new environment from a legal point of view.

You should also ascertain what legal services your corporation will provide, both before and after your move. Will the company assist you in finding legal counsel, even if the company does not foot the bill?

Countless stories can be related about legal entangle-

ments expatriates encountered because of lack of knowledge of the local laws. Everyone who has spent some time
overseas probably has at least one legal tale to tell. Two
brief stories should suffice to prove that ignorance of the
law is no better an excuse abroad than at home.

This was my husband's and my first move abroad.
And now it was time for our first trip home. He had
gone on ahead, and I had been left behind, waiting
for the children to finish school.

I arrived at the airport and breathed a sigh of relief,
knowing that in a few hours we would be reunited
with our families. Everything went smoothly until
the airport officials asked me where my letter of permission was. "What letter of permission?" I asked.
The officials replied, "The letter of permission allowing you to take HIS children out of the country."

Well, I blew my lid. I screamed, argued, and finally
resorted to begging—but nothing would budge them.
Needless to say, my education had begun. I took a
later flight, after obtaining the required letter. It was
quite a shock to learn that my legal rights to my children could be withdrawn by moving abroad.

*   *   *

My father had made his career with a multinational corporation, so my sister and I grew up in
countries other than the United States. It was a life
style I took to quite easily, so it came as no surprise to
anyone that I married a native of another country.
What did come as a shock was that when we gave
birth to our first child and I went to register him as an
American citizen, the application was rejected. I had
lost my U.S. citizenship! Neither my parents nor I
had been aware of the fact that you can lose your na-

tionality if you don't live in the United States for a specific period of time in your youth.

Have You Had All Your Shots?

Living in a foreign land may necessitate renewing or initiating immunizations against diseases you do not normally come into contact with in the United States. Again, your company should provide you with information concerning required immunizations. You will need to know which immunizations are necessary, how long they are considered to be valid, and where you can receive them. You will also need to know what documents or proofs of inoculation are required. Make sure that you've been given proper instructions on how to fill out all forms. Many expatriates have completed a series of immunizations and suffered stiff arms only to find upon their arrival that they had to be reinoculated because their papers were not correctly filled out or because particular shots were supposed to be given in more than one dose.

Sanitary conditions vary from country to country, and extra measures to protect your family's health are often wise. Check with your doctor and the U.S. Department of Health to see which shots are recommended even if they are not required. Find out what the American embassy in your new area recommends for its staff and determine if you wish your family to follow the same policy.

Also, if any member of your family is on special medication or a diet, make sure that what you need will be available where you are going. You may have to carry a year's supply of special medicine with you. You should also ensure that you have whatever documents your new host country requires for the medicines you carry.

Who Should Be Notified of Your Move?

The sooner you notify others of your move, the smoother the move will be. Some of the people and services you may wish to contact include: magazines, newspapers, book clubs, record clubs, professional journals; the Veterans Administration, the Social Security Administration, your local draft board; lawyers, accountants, stock brokers, insurance companies; licensing bureaus, professional organizations, medical personnel and services; utilities, swimming pool services, delivery services, schools, churches, local post office, friends and relatives.

What about Banking?

Your company may regard your banking and financial services needs as purely your responsibility. We recommend that you not close all of your U.S. bank accounts or that you open an account with a bank that is prepared to provide you with the services you need in the United States and abroad. There are numerous reasons for this: you may need money in the States to pay bills; your bank account can provide an immediate financial reference; and you may be paid in dollars and may need a deposit account. There are banks that offer expatriate banking services, have worldwide consumer networks and provide comprehensive service packages, including such things as time deposits, foreign currency deposits and credit. Take the time to identify your potential needs and find a bank that can fulfill them before you move.

CHAPTER VI

Real Estate at Home and Abroad

WHEN YOU MOVE ABROAD, it is usually a nonpermanent assignment. This gives rise to what must be the most frequently asked question about an international move: "What should I do with my home?" Of course, if you live in a rented house or apartment it is a simple matter of terminating your lease. But if you own your home you have two basic options: keep it or sell it.

Your Stateside House

If you can afford to keep your home in the States, by all means do so. Believe it or not, most people can. Most major corporations encourage their employees not to sell, and many corporations structure their benefit programs accordingly. Your company may be willing to pay for some or all of the following expenses:

—Real estate agent commissions for locating tenants (commissions are typically ten percent of the first year's rent and five percent on renewals; or one month's rent for the first year, and half a month's rent on renewals).

—Legal fees for the drafting of leases.

—Management fees (typically six percent to ten percent of the rent) paid to agents who watch over your property while you are overseas.

—Mortgage interest, maintenance, insurance, and taxes for up to three months if you have not found a tenant by the time you leave the country.

One often cited reason for keeping your house is the simple fact that you may not be able to afford to buy it back when you return. Horror stories abound regarding the executive who thought that he had made a killing on the sale of his home when he transferred overseas, only to find that his investment of the profits had not kept pace with the appreciation in real estate.

Another reason to keep your house rather than sell it is more emotional than economic. Your house is your home, no matter where you are living. You may be in Dubai or Frankfurt, but psychologically your home is still on Mainstreet, U.S.A. The house may be your "roots" or place to retreat if anything should go wrong. It's a point of focus and comfort for your children, knowing that they have a familiar place to return to when Mom and Dad's overseas assignment finally comes to an end.

One of our children lived in a yellow house in the States for only six months before moving overseas. But for the next seven years, he talked of his home as the "yellow house." When he returned, the house and his bedroom were half the size they had been in his mind's eye, but the image had served a very important role for him as a security blanket for seven years.

Finally, the economics of maintaining your home and renting it are quite attractive on an aftertax basis, particularly if your company offers any or all of the benefits mentioned previously. Even if you have to go it alone, keeping your home may still be an attractive option because of tax provisions for depreciation and capital gains deferral. If you want more information, contact a licensed, professional real estate management company.

Should You Ever Sell Your Home?

On the flip side of the record, there are certain circumstances in which it is probably advisable to sell your home rather than keep it. These may or may not apply to your particular situation.

If your home is carrying a 14% to 18% mortgage, it may not be possible to make ends meet, given the high cost of living overseas. In this case you should look down the road a year or two to determine if the economics of keeping your home are likely to improve with time—as a function of salary increases or higher rental income.

If you believe it is unlikely that you will return to the same city or town when your overseas assignment comes to an end, you may want to sell your home and buy another as a rental property in order to stay in the real estate market. This would enable you to move into, sell, or trade your appreciated property when you return.

If your current home is a "white elephant" or is in a depressed area that is unlikely to appreciate or is likely to be in need of costly improvements in the near future, it may be preferable to sell your home and buy a more manageable property before going overseas.

If you intend to purchase a home overseas, it may be necessary to sell your home in the States in order to come up with the required down payment. While this usually has the advantage of capital gains tax deferment, there are the other factors noted above to consider before making such a decision.

Housing Overseas

In the majority of cases, expatriates find themselves as tenants rather than owners of their new abodes. Renting your new home abroad can be no different than locating a rental in the States—or it can be quite different. It all depends upon the country you are in. While many of the same home-hunting principles apply, you may find familiar support systems (multiple listing) lacking or local practices ("key money") bewildering. Don't despair! If you keep your inquisitive spirit charged, your sense of humor high, and your walking shoes handy, you'll survive. Just remember that every expatriate in your new location has navigated this course—and that's a good place to start.

Begin your search by talking with people who have already been through it; the more recently, the better. Ask them what they did, how they did it, what they learned, and how they made their decisions. Also ask them what mistakes they made and what they would do over again, if they had the opportunity of starting from scratch.

Once again, don't forget to make lists: a list of your family's needs and preferences, a list of what is mandatory and what is optional, and a list of what other expatriates learned before and after they made their decisions. Later on you'll need a list of what's available in the market.

Armed with the experience of others, it's time to begin your search. In some locations, you will not have a choice.

Your only option may be to live in a compound; or, as is frequently the case in government service, your house may already be designated for you. In other instances the entire city awaits you.

Typically, real estate agents are more than willing to assist you for a fee. One of your first decisions will be to select a reliable agent. This may not be as easy as it sounds. In many nations there are no licensing requirements to be met or governmental agencies overseeing the business practices of those who claim to be realtors. Therefore, try to select an agent who is recommended by your company or someone you know. Previous satisfactory performance is the best recommendation that can be made.

If your company provides no assistance and realtors don't exist, the search will be entirely up to you. You may have to peruse the newspapers, contact the embassy, women's clubs, and churches, or literally go door to door asking if anything is available. Typically, the concierge will know what apartments are for rent in his building as well as in the surrounding neighborhood. More than a few of the wives in our survey resorted to this process. Whichever method you use, just remember to persevere and don't get depressed. Eventually you will succeed.

Location is a key factor. The home, office, and school should be the perimeters of your search. In many cities you'll find small enclaves of expatriates clustered in specific locales. Many families opt for these areas, sometimes known as "American ghettoes." Here life is frequently made easier by shopkeepers, repairmen, beauticians, and other service industries accustomed to catering to the needs of foreigners. As such, these locations are more geared to the tastes and mannerisms of expatriates living abroad. For these very same reasons, many people choose not to live in expatriate enclaves. They much prefer to live among the local population, as "locals." Whichever location you choose, keep in mind one very important factor: the decision should be acceptable to all the members of your family.

Once you've determined the neighborhood in which you'd like to live, the next decision is selecting a house or apartment. As you'll soon find, housing abroad runs the gamut. Some homes would be the envy of your friends in the States, while others would certainly not. What's important to remember is that almost anything is livable on a temporary basis. If what you are looking for is not available, accept that fact and make the best of it. Although housing may not be what you're accustomed to in the States, the majority of the wives we surveyed felt that their new homes were quite comparable in comfort to their stateside homes. Expatriates may have to sacrifice suburbia for apartments in the city, but few believe their standards of living decline in any meaningful way.

As you will most likely be renting rather than owning, you should be aware of the advantages and disadvantages. One key to this is enlisting the aid of a good lawyer prior to signing any lease agreement. As it will probably be in the local language and filled with the proverbial "fine print," here are some words to the wise:

—Have the lease translated into English by someone in whom you have complete confidence.
—Include a "diplomatic clause" allowing you to break the lease if you are transferred.
—Negotiate a renewal clause at a fixed rate of increase for future years.
—Establish who will be responsible for repairs as well as cosmetic improvements to the premises while you are in residence.
—If you have a pet, be sure to have the landlord's agreement, in writing, that this is acceptable.
—Clearly establish what the landlord will be responsi-

ble for providing in terms of heat, water, electricity, telephone, taxes, and the like.

Should You Buy Overseas?

You may be tempted to buy a house overseas in order to obtain the type of house you want, or to be in the right neighborhood or school district. Buying overseas is even more tempting if your company provides you with a tax-free housing allowance that would permit you to own the house for little more than the down payment. Why should you pay rent for three or four years and have nothing to show for it when it is time to move on? Well, before making such a decision, you should take note of the following considerations:

First, you should evaluate the potential gain or loss that might result from a swing in the foreign exchange rate. One maxi-devaluation or a series of mini-devaluations could wipe out half the dollar value of your down payment and capital appreciation. Conversely, a major re-valuation could double your money overnight. You will be betting on your ability to predict the strength of the U.S. dollar and the weakness of the local currency.

Second, you should evaluate the types of mortgages and levels of interest rates in your foreign country. Many overseas banks offer variable interest rate mortgages, which might appear affordable today (given your housing allowance) but which could also rise from 10% to 15% to 20% to 30%. You could end up being forced to sell your new home for lack of funds. Historical trends in inflation rates are not particularly accurate indicators during these uncertain times. Try to ascertain whether there are legally binding limits on how far and fast your interest rate can be increased.

The third factor that you should evaluate is the current

and future state of the real estate market in your foreign location. Is it currently at a high but moving higher, or is it just about to drop? Is it at a low and overdue for a rapid rise; or is it likely to fall farther before bottoming out? As in the United States, foreign real estate markets go through cycles in which housing costs rise and fall as a function of numerous variables—including the state of the economy, inflation, interest rates, mortgage availability, new construction, and simple supply and demand economics.

Last, but most important, the liquidity of an investment in a house overseas is a critical consideration. You probably won't be able to pick the date of your next assignment (be it back to the United States or other overseas posting). To be saddled with a home that does not sell in London when your company wants you in Caracas by next Monday is an awful economic and psychological dilemma. How do you set up a home in Caracas when all your cash is tied up in London? Does your family stay behind until the London house is sold? Will you have to take a major loss in order to effect a quick sale? In which country should you start the kids in school?

Unless you are experienced in the dynamics of real estate, expect your overseas assignment to last more than a few years, and have the financial resources to weather the storm if your projections are wrong, the best advice that we can offer is: keep your house in the States and rent overseas.

What If You Do Buy Your Overseas House?

If you do decide to purchase your overseas home, you can minimize your risk by taking out the largest mortgage that your housing allowance will sustain in the local currency. By minimizing the dollar-denominated down payment, you insulate yourself against the vagaries of foreign exchange-rate fluctuations. As you will be buying and selling in the local currency, the dollar value and its rate of exchange will only be relevant to the extent that you have had to use dollars in the transaction. If foreign exchange and interest rates move in your favor and if your foreign assignment lasts long enough to encompass substantial appreciation in local real estate, you could make a significant profit. And you will be doing so with a housing allowance that might otherwise have been lost forever on rent. However, since the opportunity to do this is not equal in all expatriate locations and since the risk of illiquidity is real and makes employees less mobile, most companies discourage the use of their housing allowances in this fashion. Nonetheless, buying an overseas home is a personal investment decision on the employee's part. The temptation to "take the risk" is obvious.

Bear in mind the fact that a number of variables can adversely affect your position as a homeowner in another country. Your company may reduce your housing allowance because of changes in inflation rates in the U.S. or foreign location. You may be unable to get a fixed-rate mortgage from your lending bank and, therefore, your payments could increase drastically. You could be reassigned and have to leave the country, causing your bank to recall your mortgage loan.

In all of this there is one very important caveat: *Be sure to check the legal and tax implications of your decision, whatever it may be, with your tax, accounting, financial, and legal advisors—in terms of both U.S. and foreign laws.*

CHAPTER VII

Finding a Mover

YOU MAY OR MAY NOT HAVE A CHOICE in selecting your
mover. For any number of reasons, your company
might request that you use a specific moving company. On
the other hand, you might have to contact, hire, and follow through with the moving company on your own. Personal recommendations and the Better Business Bureau
are good sources for locating a competent mover.

When we were due to be transferred home, three
moving companies were asked to estimate our move.
Understandably our company wanted to accept the
lowest bid. However, I had heard so many good reports about one of the other, larger and more expensive movers that I really felt it might be best to go
with them. I liked what I'd heard about their punc-
tuality, attention to customs details, high quality
packing material, and overall genuine concern for
family treasures.

Although we had to pay for the difference in cost,
my choice of shipper proved doubly rewarding. Our

belongings arrived in good shape and in only a little over three weeks' time. Friends from the same foreign city had moved out the same day we had and to the neighboring town, but their shipment took almost two and a half months. Bigger may not always be better, but I really felt that the larger company was more experienced in expediting the necessary papers and understood the importance of quantity and quality packing materials.

Estimates

As with each step of your move, have your list of questions ready when the estimators arrive. Questions that should be included are:

—Who is responsible for the packing and unpacking?
—How long will it take to pack our household belongings?
—What type of packing materials will be used?
—Exactly what will I be charged for?
—When and how are moving company costs to be paid?
—Will there be customs duties or taxes?
—How and when will these customs charges by paid, and by whom?
—How much and what type of insurance is provided by the moving company?
—Who is responsible for arranging for the insurance?
—What types of transportation will be used?
—What is the route by which the goods will be shipped?
—What documents will the moving company need at border crossings?

—Will there be a need to store your goods while they are in transit?

—Where will the goods clear customs?

—Who is responsible for the paperwork?

—How long will it take for your belongings to reach their destination?

Charges

You could be charged for any or all of the following: cubic footage, weight, packing materials, distance, assembling and disassembling, picking up carpets, packing and unpacking, number of pieces, value of goods, type of transportation, special services, storage, exclusive use of van, van or container days, and man hours.

Ask what you are being charged for and *get it in writing.*

What Types of Transportation Will Be Used?

A few companies will move an employee's entire shipment by air; but because of the astronomical cost, this is rare. Air transport usually occurs when there is no other alternative or in an emergency.

Goods are typically put into wooden shipping crates or a single overseas shipping container and transported by train, truck, and ship. Each method has its advantages. Remember every move is different, and what works for one move may not work for another.

If your shipment is containerized, try to have exclusive use of the shipping container. The fewer times a shipment has to be opened the better off you will be.

What About the Packing Materials?

How your belongings are packed and the kind of packing materials used are extremely important in an overseas move. If you do your own packing, check and recheck your insurance policy. Goods packed by their owners are often not covered under standard moving policies. It is best to have experienced movers do the packing; restrain yourself from helping, and merely supervise the process.

Whether you pack yourself or the movers do it for you, make sure everything is packed properly. It is foolish to skimp on packing materials.

Packing materials and procedures do vary from country to country, and you will have to be flexible. A number of tried and true suggestions, which have lessened damages, both physical and personal, are:

—Boxes should be of sturdy double-walled cardboard and secured with reinforced moving tape or heavy masking tape.

—Wooden boxes and crates are expensive, but not when the option is having to replace costly antiques or art.

—Specifically designed wardrobe boxes, dish barrels, mattress cartons, and book boxes are most desirable.

—Corrugated cardboard strips and bubble paper are excellent for packing breakables.

—Clean paper should be used to wrap dishes and glassware.

—Blanket paper, quilted padding, and heavy cloth should be used for protection and cushioning.

—Plastic coverings or cellophane should be used with caution. This type of material can collect moisture and cause water damage. However, clear plastic bags can be used to keep things clean and in sets.

—Pack heavy items in small boxes. Never overpack a container.

—When disassembling anything, place all screws, nuts, and bolts in an envelope or plastic bag and tape it inside the piece of furniture or appliance.

—If you have the space and know your overseas assignment is temporary, keep your packing materials for your departure from the host country.

—Never pack flammable products.

—Wrap silver in flannel cloth, soft cloth, or unprinted plain paper to avoid dents and scratches.

—Put a few bars of soap in with the linens to create a fresh aroma.

—Mirrors and glass picture frames should be taped to prevent cracking.

—Put coffee grounds, charcoal briquets, baking soda, or silica gel in your refrigerator and freezer to help avert mold build up.

—Candles may melt in the heat of a moving van.

—Light bulbs may explode when moving to different altitudes.

Timing Your Move

Timing is everything, as the saying goes. In most nationwide moves people tend to move during a term break in the school calendar or just before the start of school in September. This allows for the quick transition of children. However, most of the mothers we surveyed preferred the summer for the international moving process. It is better, they discovered, to do your hotel living (sometimes for months) without the added demands and constraints of school. Also by shipping your belongings to your new home at the start of the summer, you can have time to visit with relatives and friends, thus shortening the actual hotel-living stage.

Many of our respondents also recommended that you ship your household effects and stay in a hometown hotel until a week or so prior to the shipment's arrival date. You and your family may be much more content with friends and familiar routines and activities that make the time pass more quickly. On the other hand, those of our respondents without children or with children of preschool age preferred to move at off-peak times or seasons. They felt they got more attention and better service and avoided delays at country borders.

Another consideration in timing is the weather. Moving damage can often be attributed to weather conditions en route or in delivery. It stands to reason that if you insist on moving during the monsoon season, something will get wet. Also, if the ship carrying your container or crates has to weather out a hurricane, the heaving and rocking will cause some damage no matter how well things are packed. If you must move during the peak moving season or during a period of expected bad weather, then don't consider the inevitable delays and damage to your belongings the fault of the shipper. Shippers obviously try to do the best they can. They are not responsible for acts of nature. If you have a choice, pick your timing carefully. It can make your move that much better.

What Should You Know About Pickup and Delivery Dates?

The pickup date for your shipment is child's play compared to the delivery date. Most moving companies are fairly prompt—barring strikes, overwork, or inclement weather—in picking up a shipment on the agreed-upon date. Most movers do the best they can. Most will also take the initiative to notify you if they can't carry out their end of the bargain. Be aware, though, that you may legitimately be given a time span for the pickup date rather than a specific date.

Your experiences for pickup and drop-off dates will vary from country to country. If you happen to be destined for a country that functions with an "it can be done tomorrow" attitude, your anticipated delivery dates can stretch from days into weeks and even, though rarely, into months. Be emotionally and financially prepared for any turn of events. Unforeseen obstacles can arise unexpectedly, delaying the departure and/or arrival of your belongings. Be patient with your shipper, also, as the cause of delay may be beyond his control.

Our furniture took four months to reach us because an attempt was made on the part of our host country government to clean up the corruption in the customs department. The entire border was closed for months while an investigation was conducted. Meanwhile, we waited and waited.

* * *

Red tape! Red tape! And more red tape! We couldn't get the right papers to get our furniture into the country. It got to a point when we were really more amused than annoyed by the delays. At one point we were entitled to bring in five Mercedes Benzes (we couldn't even afford one) but not a single stick of our furniture! It took nine months before we ever saw our things.

What Are Special Services?

Special services can be any number of things. They are usually the requests you make that do not generally fall within the moving company's normal contract terms. You can expect that any special request will not be done as a favor but will be done at your expense. Transport companies are profit-oriented businesses. The disconnection and reinstallation of major appliances and television antennas, the pulling-up and laying-down of carpets, the hanging of draperies and pictures are all examples of special services. Large moving companies may have people on staff or will be able to recommend a service person if you have any specific needs to be fulfilled, as exemplified here:

We moved with one of the larger moving companies when we were transferred. I did not realize how important this was until we reached our destination. I didn't know a soul and was grateful for the concern of the moving company. They had an English-speaking representative who recommended a wealth of service people to help me get our home together and functioning—plumbers, electricians, carpenters, and even a fencer to make a dog run.

What Should Your Moving Contract Include?

You will be signing a contract that authorizes the mover to ship your goods. Read and understand every detail that is included. More important, know what should be included. Make sure the following are part of your moving contract:

—Shipper's name, address, telephone number.

—Authorized mover's name, address, telephone number.
—Packing dates.
—Pickup date.
—Delivery date.
—Packing procedures.
—Packing materials.
—Location of weigh scale.
—Modes of transportation.
—Special services.
—Identification or registration numbers.
—Estimated charges.
—Method of payment.
—Notification of charges.
—Claim procedures.
—Inventory list.
—Insurance, and
—Authorized signatures.

Moving Documents

The documents that will be necessary for transportation of your household goods will vary from country to country and moving company to moving company. You may have to send some documents ahead of your goods. Others you will have to hand carry. You may also need to have your documents translated into at least one other language. The following list should serve as a guideline to the types of papers you will need:

—Bills of lading: steamship, railroad, airway, truck.
—Delivery receipts.
—Freight bills.
—Insurance certificates.
—Import invoices.

—Lists of baggage for customs control.
—Packing lists, and
—Property damage claim forms.

Documents may have to be notarized. Besides this, your new country of residence may require that you file all information with its nearest consulate or embassy office. A specified number of copies may also be required, and these may have to be in English and the official language(s) of the host country as well as of the countries en route to that destination.

Your moving company, your company's representative, or the host country embassy should be able to supply you with the necessary information as to document requirements (and possibly the documents themselves). In the final analysis, though, it is your responsibility to make sure you have all the necessary paperwork completed.

CHAPTER VIII

Getting Ready for the Movers

I F YOU HAVE DONE YOUR HOMEWORK, getting ready for the packers and shipper will be that much easier. With your notes and lists in hand, your efforts during packing will be better organized and more purposeful. Guesswork and uncertainty will be cut in half. While you may not appreciate this until you have arrived and unpacked at your destination, the sum of your labors will ultimately be realized.

What Goes? What Stays? What Gets Thrown Out?

The answer to this question is entirely up to you. There are those who hate excess baggage and will jump at the opportunity to discard unnecessary items. Conversely, there are those who cling to every possession in hopes that one day it will serve a useful purpose.

Although a move usually provides the perfect opportunity to discard worn-out items, the women who took part in our survey agreed that a move is not the time to get rid of your husband's favorite, though somewhat tattered, easy chair or your daughter's scruffy teddy bear. Such beloved belongings ease the transition and make a foreign land seem more like home. The familiarity of your own things reinforces the security and comfort of the family no matter where your home may be. This is especially true when children are involved. The disruption of what is familiar to them is often traumatic and stressful. Moving from one town to another, or even from one side of the United States to the other, means household goods reach their destination in days. International moves take considerably longer and intensify the family's emotional turbulence, as exemplified in this story.

Our six-year-old son's anguish over not having his possessions for an extended period of time became evident to us only at the time of the arrival of the shipment. Our son dashed to his room and excitedly gave his friends a guided tour, breathlessly detailing, "This is my bed where I sleep. This is my desk where I study. This is my huge basket for all my animals and this is. . . ." He continued on until he had described every last thing he owned.

What Can and Should Be Taken?

Due to host country regulations, you may only be allowed to bring in one shipment of goods and/or one product in specific categories. From your research, you may also have learned that there is not the quality, price, or availability of products as in the United States. Qualified repairmen and replacement parts do not exist in some areas of the world. And many families do not have the luxury of buying in the States between moves from one country to another. Rather, they are moved from foreign nation to foreign nation and must make do with what they have. Therefore, plan carefully what you will be shipping. As one housewife related:

> It was my second international move and I was determined that it be better than my first. At one point, I stood in my kitchen arguing with the mover about packing my lamp in the same box as my husband's anvil. He claimed that he knew what he was doing—and he couldn't understand my problem anyway, since I could collect the insurance money if the lamp were damaged. I finally convinced him to put my lamp in a different box, explaining that money is nice, but it would do me little good if I could not light my home. I knew from my premove trip that I would not easily replace my lamp at our destination.

Stock up on family favorites that will not be available: that special brand of peanut butter, chocolate, mixes of all kinds, as well as spices and condiments. Rest assured, there are tasty substitutes which your family will grow to enjoy, but your initial food supply from home helps to ease your transition. Such personal items as toothpaste, hair spray, shave creams, and make-up should not be forgotten. You may not recognize your favorite shade of hair coloring or lipstick at your destination, even if it's made by the same company and has the same name. Manufacturing standards are not the same worldwide.

Be sensible when compiling your list of what to bring. Most companies frown upon shipping five-year supplies of U.S. products. Besides, where on earth are you going to store everything? Can you use it all before the expiration dates? Ship only what you feel you simply can't do without.

Other important factors in deciding what to ship are: country restrictions, the weather, space, insurance, and your company's moving policies. Find out what items are prohibited or taxed exorbitantly by the host country, and try to live without them. Weather will also be a strong determinant of what you take. Hot, humid climates can wreak havoc on upholstered furniture, antiques, and thick rugs. Space is a definite consideration. Most multinational corporations conduct business in large cities, where housing is at a premium. You may have to condense your four-bedroom colonial into a small apartment. The age of your belongings is also important. Your antiques may not withstand a long journey and months in storage. Some moving companies will not insure items of extreme value, and it may also be impossible to get insurance coverage in your new location. You might prefer to leave your treasured or uninsurable items with trusted friends, relatives, or a reliable storage company.

Which appliances you take will depend on your new country's electrical current, which may differ from that of the States. Europe, for example, is on a 220–240 volt, 50-cycle system, whereas the United States is on a 110–120 volt, 60-cycle system. This is particularly important when thinking about taking a microwave or personal computer; check with your appliance manufacturers.

There are ways to overcome voltage difficulties. You can use step-down transformers for small appliances. For large appliances, a high-capacity transformer can be installed at your new home's main switch box. Voltage regulators are also recommended, as high currents, low currents, brownouts, and blackouts can damage electrical appliances. Televisions manufactured in the United States might not receive the images transmitted by your host country stations, as screen lineages do differ. You would probably do well to buy or rent a locally made television after your move.

Another consideration is that American plugs will not fit into many foreign wall sockets. Prongs can be round, short, thick, flat, and angled, or the plugs may be three pronged. There are two easy solutions to this problem. One is to have an electrician present within the first few days of moving in with sufficient plugs to convert all your appliances. A second is to purchase adaptor plugs. Remember, *neither of these solutions is a method for adapting to higher currents.* If you plug a 110-volt appliance into a 220-volt outlet, you will burn out the motor. Become familiar with the basic terminology of volts, watts, amperes, and cycles, and make sure you have sufficient transformer capacity.

Many electrical appliance manufacturers have international divisions. Call and ask them if your appliances can be serviced and parts secured in your new locale. Determine if your guarantees and warranties will be recognized and honored overseas. Note that in some foreign countries it is a criminal offense to repair or supply parts for products manufactured outside the country's borders. Two suggestions: buy the least complicated appliances and obtain schematic drawings for them. The simpler the product, and the fewer the dials, the less chance something will break. Schematic drawings provide several advantages. They will help local repairmen obtain substitute parts and determine how to repair your machine. The drawings can also be valuable if you have to request that parts be sent to you from the United States.

The cost of electricity in many countries might make it more profitable to sell some of your present electrical appliances and purchase gas-run appliances. Gas, though, is not without its problems. Appliances may have to be adjusted and you might have to invest in an individual gas tank. But, on the whole, gas tends to be cheaper and more easily obtainable than electricity in many countries outside the United States.

To assist you in making your appliance decisions, send for: "Electric Current Abroad," U.S. Government Printing Office, Washington, DC 20202.

Last-Minute Shopping

Use your research and your friends' suggestions when compiling your shopping list. There are a number of items that you should carefully consider; they include: air conditioners, humidifiers, or dehumidifiers; automobiles; any and all bathroom fixtures; carpeting; any and all electrical light fixtures; infant and baby equipment; kitchen appliances (including a freezer), oven and refrigerator/freezer thermometers; washer and dryer; tools; any and all types of storage units; holiday ornaments; hobby supplies; dictionary, thesaurus, encyclopedia, atlas, and world almanac.

The major consideration in doing your shopping should be the cost effectiveness of stateside purchasing and subsequent overseas transport versus local availability, purchase, and transport.

Another word to the wise. Allow yourself an extra day or so for last-minute shopping as it is not uncommon, according to the survey, to be asked to make purchases for fellow employees. Everything from major appliances to disposable diapers are frequently requested by others already stationed abroad. When buying for others, however, be prepared for problems. Although most people are reasonable, there are those who will take advantage of you and the company. Some tips which should be useful include:

—Check with your husband's supervisor to see if you are allowed to put anything in your shipment for another family.

—Although this may sound crass, get the cash up front. Many people have been stuck with the bill for favors they did for others.

—Agree to purchase only what is convenient to your time schedule.

—Check to make sure no requested item is on a contraband list. Contraband could hold up your shipment in customs indefinitely.

—Make sure the request is specific: sizes, colors, serial numbers, price range. More than one expatriate has good naturedly purchased an item only to be told that it is not suitable, too expensive, or no longer wanted.

What Should Be Stored?

Some companies prefer that their employees store their household furnishings. Some of these companies provide furniture and appliance allowances. other companies may maintain furnished homes or a warehouse in the host country where employees can go to choose the furnishings they wish. Storing your belongings in the United States may be advantageous if your stay abroad will be short term or if you will be moving to smaller quarters.

Inventories

When moving overseas, months may pass between the time your goods leave the United States and arrive at the new destination. Consequently, it is imperative that you make a detailed inventory. There are several different ways you can go about this. If you leave it entirely in the hands of the mover, you can expect a less detailed description. Cartons may simply be marked "miscellaneous" or under such catch-all headings as clothing, tools, or medical supplies. It will be very difficult when filling out a claim form eight months after the move to recall whether you owned two shovels or three. Although we would all like to believe that we possess infallible memories, it is best to rely on a list.

Some people like to make a room-by-room inventory. Everything that belongs in the living room is listed under that heading. This type of inventory can be time consuming, but it will save time at your destination and make it easier to settle into your new home. As all cartons will be labeled according to the room in which they belong, it will be simple to direct the movers in placing the cartons in the appropriate place.

You can also use a camera to take your inventory. This method, too, can be time consuming and expensive; and it definitely has to be completed well in advance of the arrival of the movers. However, a photographic inventory is especially useful for such valuable items as antique furniture, jewelry, and art.

Some people prefer to take their inventory as they are packing or being packed. Although this method has been successfully employed, it, too, has its drawbacks. Unforeseen interruptions can occur, which can ultimately result in a partial listing, or you might find moving so rushed that you lack the time to make a complete list. The advantage to this method, however, is that you will know exactly what is in every single carton.

An accurate inventory can assist you in avoiding excessive customs duties as well as facilitate you in making insurance claims if necessary. Your inventory can also be an aid for arranging your furnishings in your new home.

All inventories, regardless of the type you choose, should include item names, quantities, ages, and values. Estimate the total worth of small items that are not individually listed. They are all worth something, and you would be amazed how quickly the little items add up to a significant figure.

Whether or not you have done an inventory, your mover is also responsible for compiling one. Make sure that you are in agreement as to the condition of your belongings and the number of cartons that are being shipped or stored. If you disagree with the mover's notations regarding the condition of your goods, indicate this disagreement in writing on the shipper's inventory list before you sign it. Make sure you receive a copy of the mover's list before the van leaves your premises.

Valuing Your Goods

If you are destined to a life of successive international moves, develop a file of receipts for your furniture and other household goods. If you can present a bill for an item, it is much easier to establish the value of a loss for your insurance company. If you have inherited or received valuable gifts, it may be worth paying for an appraisal before your move. Hire qualified experts whose appraisals will be accepted by your insurance company. You may also want to revise the appraisals periodically, as many items increase in value annually.

What Types of Insurance Will Be Needed?

You will need to know and understand exactly what type of coverage you should have for the belongings you will be shipping, the personal items you will be carrying with you, and those you intend to store. You may also need: auto insurance, both for the car(s) you leave behind and the car(s) you have in your new country; house insurance, for your house in the States as well as your overseas home; property insurance, for your belongings while you reside in a hotel or other form of temporary housing; office building insurance; school bus insurance; car rental insurance; life insurance; and pet insurance.

Determine who is responsible for taking out your insurance policies: you, the moving company, the home office, or the overseas office. Regardless of who is responsible, you will need to know exactly what the various policies cover: when the coverage begins and ends; what claims you can make; how you make the claims; and when the claims deadlines are. Don't assume these matters will be automatically taken care of by others, as this family did:

She was seated on the stairs of the language school, a woman in her late forties. She was totally oblivious to the people around her. She sat steadfast, staring into space as tears streamed down her cheeks.

Eventually, I sat next to her and said, "Can I help you?" She began to sob hysterically. Finally she said, "Yesterday my husband and I received our shipment. We can't believe it. Almost everything was saturated with water and mold. I think my husband is going to have a nervous breakdown. We don't have any insurance. My husband thought the company took care of the insurance, and I thought my husband took care of it. I just don't know what we are going to do."

Fortunately, the English-speaking community rallied round the family and most of the lost household items were either donated or provided at discounts. Don't let this happen to you. Read every document carefully and double check that all arrangements have been made.

Should You Take Your Pet?

In many countries having a pet will present no problem at all, but in others you will be strongly advised against it. To leave your pet behind can be a very sad experience; but to have your pet quarantined for as much as six months may be sadder still. England, for example, requires that all pets be quarantined in a British kennel for six months. Visitation rights are granted the owners, but it is difficult for owner and pet to see each other in this manner. Your pet has no way of understanding why he or she must endure such an extended separation. Some animals are so emotionally traumatized by the quarantine that they never recover. Think twice before subjecting your pet to this experience.

Investigate the restrictions and requirements for pets entering your new homeland. The proper permits and inoculation records must be in order. Be careful here, as in many instances the permits and inoculations are valid only for short periods of time. It is just as important to know the laws that apply to your pet as it is to know the laws that apply to you.

Scheduling the departure, length of travel time, and arrival are also extremely important. Check with the carrier well in advance to make arrangements for your animal's passage. Also remember that confined travel is emotionally stressful to your pet. You might want to use animal sedatives. Remember to label your pet's container in the languages of all countries transited as well as that of your destination. And don't forget to use the words "LIVE ANIMAL."

Never arrange for an animal to arrive late at night or on a weekend. Your pet, too, must clear customs or be examined by a veterinarian before it can be released. If the proper authorities are not present when your pet arrives, he or she may be neglected for hours, even days.

For those of you who will be shipping your pet through New York, Kennedy Airport has an animalport run by the ASPCA. This service is available twenty-four hours a day, every day of the year. It can handle any animal and is responsible for medical examinations, cleaning, feeding, watering, and exercising your animal. This is not an automatic service. You must arrange for it. If you send a self-addressed, stamped envelope, the Animalport will send you its publication, "Tips for Traveling With Your Pet." The address is: ASPCA Animalport, Air Cargo Center, Kennedy International Airport, Jamaica, NY 11430. Telephone (718) 656-6042.

Information on the transportation of your pet can be obtained from state health departments, foreign consulates, and the ASPCA. The address for the New York ASPCA is: ASPCA, 441 East 92nd Street, New York, NY 10028. Telephone: (212) 876-9700.

Hand carry all the documents relating to your pet. If you plan to have your pet in temporary housing with you, you will need to pack your pet's necessities as well.

CHAPTER IX

Countdown to Moving Day

FINAL PREPARATIONS OF YOUR HOME for the move should be made before the packers arrive. Remove pictures, brackets, racks, lights, and anything else that is going with you from the walls and ceilings. Wash and clean as much as possible. Service and repair belongings in need or almost in need. Also order any spare parts that may be necessary as it's much easier to do this in a community where you know your way around and are familiar with the repair people.

Get rid of everything you don't want well ahead of time. Packing day is not the time to hold a garage sale or make deliveries to friends or charities, nor do you want undue distractions such as having to converse with Cousin Mary when she stops by for her plants. Take what is going to be traveling with you to your hotel or to a friend's house. A baby's favorite toy or blanket packed by mistake can get the entire move off to a bad start.

If you have decided to pack according to room, put your

belongings in the same room they will be going to in your new home. For example, that old mirror from your mother-in-law, which is now hanging in the living room but which you plan to put in your bedroom in the new house, should be placed in and labeled "master bedroom."

Make sure that all utilities and appliances are disconnected. It can be costly if packers must wait for an appliance serviceman to arrive. In fact, arrange for disconnections to take place several days in advance. Last-minute laundry can always be done at a local laundromat or at a friend's or relative's house. However, make sure that telephone and electrical or gas services are not terminated until your departure. These may be needed right up to the last minute.

Packing

The cardinal rule to remember is: *Devote yourself to one task at a time and do it well.*

If you are lucky enough to be given an orientation or language course, arrange your schedule so the course doesn't conflict with the packing schedule. While you are supervising the packing, *any potential disruption should be taken care of prior to the packing days.* Cancellation of any services, any financial transactions, medical exams for your family and pets, or returning of borrowed items should all be taken care of at another time. Avoid any errand that will take you away from the house.

Two final tips: have coffee and sodas on hand for the packers; it's a welcome gesture. Also, if you can possibly arrange it, don't plan to sleep in the house during the last few nights of packing. It's nice to go off someplace and get away from the clutter. It rejuvenates the mind and body and will give you strength for the next day.

Should You Label Your Belongings?

Yes! Yes! Yes! Moving internationally can become a three-ring circus without a system for identifying your wrapped and boxed goods. Most families find they really have four separate shipments: goods to be hand carried and used in their temporary residence, goods to be air freighted, goods that will form the major part of the move, and goods to be stored. Don't forget all those other stacks that you will be accumulating: the things for Cousin Erma's family, the things you wish to donate to your local charity, the treasures you wish to sell in your garage sale. Each item should be marked. (Once again you will find it invaluable to keep lists to assist you with what goes where, when, and how.)

Although everything should be marked clearly and accurately, the shipment bound for overseas is the most important when it comes to labeling. Proper labeling will save you time, confusion, and frustration.

One trick that many expatriate wives have found helpful is to obtain a vocabulary list in the foreign language and label the boxes appropriately in advance. Your movers in your new homeland may not speak a single word of English, and it will be up to you to direct the move and unpacking. If you prefer, you can also use a number or color system. With either of these systems the new words you will need to learn will be minimal. Both are simple systems that allow the movers only to look for the rooms by number or colored signs that you will have attached to the doorways.

Encourage the children to learn the foreign words for your furnishings and you will have happy helpers on delivery day. Children often enjoy being part of the move and will gladly call out the numbers or words as the crates come off the truck.

Another bit of information to keep in mind is that items

that might be tempting to anyone while your goods are in transit should be marked in code and listed on your private inventory.

You may also find that you will have to be creative in your labeling, as many countries will limit you to one of a kind of a product that they judge as being a luxury item. If you have more than one record player, for example, one could be named "record player," another "hi-fi," another "stereo."

Should Your Husband Help?

This is a question only you can answer. You know your man and yourself. One woman, who has made twelve moves in fifteen years, claims that one of her secrets to moving successfully is to keep her husband occupied elsewhere on moving day. Her advice was:

Once the moving documents are in order and signed, you should encourage your husband to leave for his new assignment well before the date the packers are due. If he cannot be out of the country during the packing days, enlist the aid of his secretary and business associates to keep him well occupied at the office so he won't even have time to consider slipping home to "help." His "executive" nature is likely to surface when he comes home and he will tend to countermand your orders or question everything you do. There's nothing worse than having him stare at you as you sort out the spices to go and those to throw—unless, of course, he takes over and throws out all the rare herbs.

Most of our respondents said that they preferred to

manage the move without their husbands. However, many families found that husband, wife, and children could work together as an efficient team. Follow your instincts and past experiences.

Should Your Children Help?

Children, even toddlers, can be useful and helpful, and should be made to feel a part of the move. Children seem to cope better if they are allowed to participate. They can sort out their belongings—throwing out broken items, giving away the unwanted and outgrown, and boxing or bagging games and toys so that little pieces won't be lost. When you child's attention span wears out, it's time to let him or her go off to play with friends or visit relatives.

What's Next?

The movers have departed, your home has been readied for its new residents, and all the loose ends of the family's life are now in a semblance of order. It is time to move on. An experienced expatriate wife will tell you that this is the only lull in the stages of moving and it should be looked upon as luxury time for you and your family. Take advantage of it . . . rest up and recharge your mental and physical batteries for what lies ahead.

In traveling to your new home, if possible, plan your route so that you will have an opportunity to visit relatives and friends that you may not see again for a while. Or simply plan to stop along the way at a resort that appeals to you. Indulge yourselves for a few days. The rest and relaxation will do you a world of good. It will erase exhaustion and ease the tension of the last days of farewell parties and packing. This time together as a family will also afford each member the chance to understand the others' feelings better and aid in everyone's emotional support. Soon, the family will be called upon to pull together as a team, joining forces in the coming phases of transculturation.

CHAPTER X

Countdown to Delivery Day

THE TIME BEFORE YOUR SHIPMENT ARRIVES at your new doorstep can be quite valuable. You can find your new home, if one has not been provided for you or you did not have the benefit of a premove visit. You can take care of any cleaning, painting, installations, and alterations and connections of vital services. Many of our respondents also began their language lessons at this time, finding even just a little knowledge of the new language a huge benefit. Other women mentioned that joining a new-comers club or American Women's Club shortly after they arrived in the country was of great value in helping them set up their new homes.

What Should Be Done on Delivery Day?

When your shipment of household goods arrives in the host country, excitement will fill the air as everyone in the family anticipates the luxury of sleeping in his or her own bed again. Be patient though; your belongings may be delayed at the docks or in a customs warehouse until local officials have had the chance to inspect them and check the necessary paperwork.

The actual unloading of your goods—off the truck and into your new home—can be exalting, as reported by one of our survey wives:

> We had waited five months for our shipment. The house had been freshly painted, shelves lined, curtains hung, floors washed and waxed. I had gotten up at five o'clock that morning because I was so anxious to see my furniture. Friends were standing by to help, and my husband even took the day off from work. It was exciting!

Have your inventory in hand when the container or crates arrive at your new doorstep. Have someone check off each piece. Enlist the aid of friends, relatives, husband, and co-workers. The more eyes and hands, the better. Your job will be to direct what goes where.

Try not to sign any receipts until you are in complete agreement with the agent regarding lost or damaged goods. Of course, in some countries this will not be an option for you. You will have no alternative but to sign the documents if you wish to take possession of your belongings. Be sure to note on the document any discrepancies or complaints. Keep your wits and sense of humor with you, and remember you can always make your complaints later—especially if your original inventories are in order.

Where to Begin

Unpack the radio or record player first. The music will put everyone in a good mood. Find the one box that you've specifically marked to be opened first, which contains cleaning equipment and essential kitchen supplies, such as the coffee pot. Make a point of completely unpacking and setting up one room, such as the living room, where you can retreat periodically or at day's end. The remainder of the unpacking will proceed more quickly than you've anticipated and soon you will feel comfortably settled.

Let children have a say in the arrangement and decoration of their new rooms. By all means let them unpack their own boxes. It will be like Christmas as they rediscover their toys and belongings.

What About Filing Claims?

It is your responsibility to find out when, where, to whom, and how claims are filed. Be prepared. You should make it a point to understand exactly what your shipper is liable for in the event of loss or damage. Know exactly what your corporation's insurance company and any other outside insurance agency are liable for as well. Never assume you have the type of coverage you want unless you arranged for it yourself.

Our goods were transported via ship and had to remain in storage for long periods of time at each end of the move. We thought we were covered for everything, until the insurance agent arrived. What a shock when we found out how wrong we were: the insurance policy didn't cover water damage, insect infestation, or warpage. Well, that took care of just about every article that was damaged. There was hardly a single thing that did not fall into one of the three categories. I had started out with almost new furniture and ended up with railroad salvage.

There are more cheerful insurance tales, and another story told to us was a classic:

I had moved countless times and thought I had experienced just about everything until our most recent move. We had just come from Brazil and our stuffed piranha, which had cost all of three dollars, had had its teeth knocked out. I thought the insurance company would merely reimburse me, but, hold your hats, they actually sent my piranha out and it returned to me with a complete set of uppers and lowers. Now, I really do have a conversation piece. I don't know anyone else who owns a piranha with dentures.

If you must make a claim, be prepared by having all bills of lading, exceptions to delivery, an itemized statement of the claim, a copy of a letter of claim against the carrier involved and any response from the carrier, a copy of your inventory, a copy of the packer's inventory, copies of all repair and cleaning estimates and bills, a survey report, and original invoices or appraisals for items valued at $500 or more.

PART FOUR

CHAPTER XI

Culture Shock

ONE OF THE BEST DEFINITIONS OF CULTURE SHOCK has been expressed by anthropologist Dr. Kalvero Olberg, who defined it as "an occupational disease of people who are suddenly transplanted abroad." Our own survey of international wives provided another definition: "It's that strange feeling that things are not quite right. Yet you just can't get a handle on how to make them right."

Culture shock consists of the psychological events that occur to a person in the initial phases of his or her encounter with a different culture. It is a profound learning experience, which can lead to a great degree of self-awareness and personal growth. The growth may take time and may be painful, but the results are usually worth it.

No one is immune from culture shock. It is a universal phenomenon that affects anyone who finds himself or herself in a new environment. Age, position, sex, and educational background make little difference other than, perhaps, a difference of degree.

Who Suffers Most?

Unfortunately, the wife does. As an employee, the husband usually retains his contact with the company; his tasks pose few surprises, and because of premove preparation he knows what to expect as far as differences in his working environment. Because of their natural adaptability, children tend to react quite well to change. Also, both husband and children—because of work and school respectively—spend their days performing relatively familiar tasks in familiar environments and have less time to react to disturbing cultural differences. The wife, on the other hand, is constantly exposed to the new culture while she sets about finding and running the family's new home. It falls to the wife to rebuild the daily routine and cope with the problems encountered by each of the family members, all while trying to learn a new language and adjust to her own changing role. The burden of total and overall orientation is hers, and she usually has few helping hands.

Our survey showed that the majority of women transferred abroad receive little or no formal preparation for living in the new culture. Most receive no formal assistance or counseling once the move has been made. Unlike her spouse, the wife has no bilingual secretary or subordinates to whom she can delegate tasks or direct her questions. She may be lucky enough to have a chauffeur or maid who speaks her language, but such gems are not usually provided by the company. In other words, the wife has to seek out her own support systems.

Our survey also showed that many husbands are unaware of the stress their wives are feeling. Because of premove orientation courses and cushioning provided by coworkers, husbands often cannot comprehend why their wives experience adjustment problems. It is very easy to overlook the fact that the perspectives of husbands and wives overseas are usually diametrically different.

From the onset, if you and your husband are to be successful in building your life abroad, you must share the culture-shock work load. You must be involved with each other and not be sidetracked by external distractions in the new culture and work setting. Discuss your conflicts as well as your conquests, and make sure that you spend time together, just the two of you.

What Are Some Common Symptoms?

Many of the women we talked to reported that they sometimes felt depressed, slept badly, worried, or felt restless. At times, though infrequently, they felt fearful and were unable to make decisions. They sometimes found it difficult to be alone and were unable to stick to plans. Some of the respondents mentioned overeating or loss of appetite, physical illnesses, increased smoking, daydreaming, apprehension, marital or sexual problems, difficulty in establishing friendships, and problems with the children. There are many other common symptoms of culture shock: excessive concern over cleanliness; fear of drinking water, food, dishes, and bedding, as well as fear of physical contact with servants or other local nationals; dependence on other expatriates who have lived in the host country for a long time; extreme reactions to frustrations and delays that would be perceived as minor at home; refusal to learn the language of the host country; and the conviction that all foreigners are likely to cheat, rob, or injure you.

Although the list of symptoms is long, take heart. No one person has all of these problems and fears, nor does everyone experience the same degree of stress. No matter how personal your problems may seem at a given point, rest assured that there are others who have had them too. *You are not alone.*

What Are Some Common Reactions?

Reactions to culture shock are fairly predictable. Some people flee, some people fight, and some people adapt.

One of the most drastic reactions is withdrawal. You can retreat to familiar turf, refusing to submit yourself to any psychological pressures. Or you may opt for a partial retreat by locating yourself and your family in an area that minimizes your contact with the local people and culture. "Little America" or "Gringo Gulch" are two of the terms used to describe those areas in foreign cities that become predominately American in character. The concentration of Americans comes about for many reasons: the area is near the American school, the houses are more suited to American tastes, the churches provide services in English, stores carry American products, and English-language television is available. Such areas are perpetuated by expatriates, especially those who are uncomfortable in new countries.

There are drawbacks to living in such a cultural bubble. If expatriates shop only at stores that cater to them, send their children only to American schools, join only American clubs, and make friends only with other Americans, they become so insulated from the country in which they are residing that they will never discover any of the major benefits of living abroad.

"Going native" is another reaction. Some individuals, who think they have adapted superbly, flee from their own culture by becoming totally immersed in the host culture. They live, eat, and dress as the local nationals do. They send their children to local schools and involve themselves almost exclusively with people of the host country. This kind of a reaction can be just as harmful as living in a cultural bubble; it's the other end of the spectrum. Expatriates who "go native" often experience great confusion, especially when it comes time for the next move. The problems are worse when only one member of the family chooses this type of reaction:

> My husband quickly adapted to the Latin American ways. Some might even have mistaken him for a native. However, his new personality even carried over to our home life. Instead of being his "partner" I was being spoken to and treated in much the same manner as our servants. I was sure he hadn't even realized how much he had changed, but I was determined that there would be another change. So, as I prepared for summer home leave, I explained to my husband the ways in which he had changed and said that I was unhappy with the person he had become. Two weeks alone did the trick. By the time he joined the family for his home leave he was his "old self" again.

Some people react to culture shock by taking ethnocentrism to its extreme. Unfortunately, it is this type of reaction that gives rise to the chronic complainer. We provide a description of this type of individual because he or she can do the most damage to your own attempts to adjust to the new culture.

For the chronic complainer, nothing is right with the host country while nothing is wrong with the home country. A victim of stereotypical thinking, the complainer maintains negative and prejudicial attitudes toward everything and everybody. If the complainer is a corporate wife, she probably believes that the company couldn't care less if she's alive or dead, and she may feel that the company is neglecting or mistreating her personally. For such a person, complaining is a defense mechanism, which gives solace in an incomprehensible world.

A complainer is a danger for all who come in contact with him or her. Complainers tend to be very dominant and vocal people who can create dissatisfaction in others where none had previously existed. If there is one piece of advice that you heed when you move overseas, make it this: identify the complainers and avoid them. Although complaining is used as a defense mechanism, there is little that you can do to help unless you are a professional counselor. If you spend your time with such a person, unfortunately, you will probably be drained of all your good sense and courage, and you, too, may become a complainer.

Then there are those, and we hope you will be one of them, who make the experience of living overseas one to be cherished. These people are not Pollyannas who see only the good. They are realists who seek out the positive. They, too, have been besieged by culture shock, by the daily stresses and strains of living in strange surroundings. Instead of fleeing, however, they face each new day with the realization that they will gain more knowledge about their new home and new culture, and themselves.

For many people, the knowledge that others have been in the same boat is all it takes to turn them around:

I'd heard stories of dependence on medication, tales of infidelity, and depictions of women who refused to leave the grounds of their residences while living abroad. What I encountered was as different as night is from day. I met women who were actively engaged in attaining a balance and reconciling the differences between living abroad and living at home. Never before had I met so many high-caliber,

outgoing, delightful women—who were always willing to help. These women invariably pointed out the
good things about the host culture.

Every now and then someone would become depressed and once in a while the problem would seem
magnified because of the distance from home. But,
generally speaking, these women were buoyant, high
spirited, and lots of fun to be with. They had already
learned to help each other cope with the culture
shock syndrome. They helped me immensely.

Coming to Terms with the Phases of Culture Shock

No one can tell you exactly when, or even if, you will
cease being discomforted by culture shock. The knowledge that what you are feeling is not unique, but is commonly experienced by those who move overseas, should
be comforting in and of itself. Learning how to counter-
balance normal but unpleasant reactions can lift your
morale for the duration of the adjustment process.

Normally, one enters a new culture in a fairly high state
of excitement and anticipation. For the transient, culture
shock is usually mild in comparison to what is felt by
people who know that they will be residing in "strange"
surroundings for a relatively extended period of time.
People who have just arrived in the new country, and especially those who know that their assignments are going
to be short term, are viewers rather than participators.
They look forward to the cultural differences—the dress,
the language, the food—but are insulated from the stress
of living in the host country and are not yet personally
involved in the new culture. The stresses of adjustment
may manifest themselves only in nervous fatigue, which
often results from the frustrations of neither understand-

ing nor being able to express oneself in the host country language or from efforts to catch the cues that are essential to courteous behavior in a strange society.

The next phase is characterized by active attempts to adjust to living in the new culture. During this stage the expatriate explores and often accepts the network of values, customs, and habits that are prevalent in the new environment. Many values that were once assumed to be true are subject to questioning and compared and contrasted with those of the host country. Awareness of differences and similarities is heightened. The blinders come off and a new outlook on life begins to evolve. It is during this period that people experience the most acute adjustment stresses.

For the expatriate in this phase, every aspect of life "back home" can become overly glorified. The problems and the difficulties are often forgotten, and only the best, the "good ol' days," are remembered. Repression rules the individual as he or she struggles to hold on to what he or she knows "should be" the structure of life and its expectations. Frequently, though, a solitary trip "home" alters the illusion and brings one back to reality.

Be aware of the fact that major differences are rarely the cause for concern. Rather, the constant, unrelenting, trivial disturbances—which seem to pile up until you can tolerate no more—are the straws that break the camel's back. The breakage of a favorite dish by a maid, the driver who cuts you off in traffic, the electricity that does not function during your dinner party, the lack of water for the fourth day in a row—all take on tremendous importance. The individual in this adaptive phase is very often like a time bomb set to go off, ticking away continually until that crucial moment when the explosion takes place.

At this point the expatriate wife often turns her hostility inward. She may begin to feel inadequate and become depressed. For a woman abroad this is the critical stage. It is now that she might retreat to her "home territory" or take that giant step into the final stage of adjustment. Some women do actually return home. But most, particularly those who have made more than one international move, fight the depression, knowing that after a while they will pass into the third phase.

The final phase of coming to terms with the culture sets in when the issues are brought into balance. Once the expatriate has come to terms with the new environment, there is a resurgence of optimism, interest, acceptance, and cross-cultural contact:

> For the first six months I so disliked the host country that I would have returned home in a minute if I could have gotten my hands on an airline ticket. But after a year I love it and couldn't wait to get back to it after my first home leave. After the second year I had little desire for home leave; I was content and very busy. By the end of the third year, though, I felt that I'd basically done all that I wanted to do and I was ready to move on and conquer yet another foreign assignment.

How You Can Minimize Culture Shock

The capacity to deal with the anxiety and stress of culture shock and the ability to function under new and different circumstances are skills that can be learned. The very first step is to recognize that cultural shock is a universal phenomenon. There is no set pattern as to when and in what degree any family member will be stricken. Preparation is one of the most effective means for combatting this problem. So before venturing into a new cultural environment, you and the rest of your family would be wise to use any and all resources at your disposal for learning about your prospective home. Most particularly, pay attention to the values, behavioral patterns, and communication styles of the people with whom you will come in contact. Without this knowledge you will always be an alien.

However, it is not enough to recognize that you can become a victim of culture shock or that you can help remedy the problem by knowing about the country and its people. You must, as well, know yourself and your culture. Your cultural upbringing has provided you with your road map for life. It has instructed you on the rules and behavioral patterns necessary for survival at home. It has taught you what is and is not appropriate, what is and is not rational. This cultural upbringing is your "frame of reference" in your new environs and, as such, must be recognized.

The term "cultural baggage" has been coined to indicate those modes of behavior which you carry with you from place to place around the world, by which people recognize your nationality before you've said a word. To be sure, some of that baggage is useful; but most of it is not.

As an American living abroad or contemplating moving abroad, it is imperative to realize that your cultural baggage can become a burden in your new host country. Stress, disorientation, and feelings of isolation are brought on by unfamiliar situations and complicated by a lack of awareness of cultural baggage as well as by any inability to deal with the new and different. You may tend to cope by resorting to familiar behavioral practices which are inappropriate and will not work in your new environment. It might be to your advantage to pretend that your mind is like a tape recorder and that the tape you've been living your life by can be re-recorded so that those aspects of the new culture which are fundamental to living in the new country can take the place of the old expectations and behavior patterns which are inappropriate. All you will be doing is enlarging your fund of knowledge and increasing your ability to adapt. This process is difficult and time consuming, but be patient and determined. The process of adapting can be exciting and fun, if you let it.

First, identify the specific problems. Blaming all your unhappiness on the host country, your spouse, and the company is unrealistic. Remember, *stress exists in the perceiver, not in the object or situation perceived.*

Focus on the people or occasions that make you unhappy in your new surroundings. Is it your maid? Your inability to express your requests to her? The lack of privacy you feel by having an outsider live in your home? Is it your isolation from friends and relatives? Your lack of modern conveniences? Your boredom? Whatever the problems may be, you will not be able to solve them without knowing exactly what they are.

Once you have identified the causes of your stress, set yourself specific, obtainable objectives. Make your goals reachable. "Happiness" is a rather broad and indistinct goal. Whatever is bothering you, try to bring it down to a level you can manage.

If you cannot communicate with your maid you should definitely learn to speak at least a little of the language. Even if you do not intend to become fluent, learn the terms and phrases needed to run your home. If you find having live-in help too frustrating and too much of an infringement on your privacy, opt for a day maid or none at all. If your husband's new hours are upsetting, ask him what can be done. One of our interviewees explained:

> I found it frustrating that my husband's new office hours allowed for a three-hour lunch and rest, but that the work day did not end until 8:30 p.m. With an

hour of commuting time, he never saw our children and our dinner was not until 9:30 or 10:00 p.m. With his boss's consent my husband adapted his office life to "American hours." Our family life returned to a happy norm, and the U.S. home office was so pleased that eventually the whole regional office went to "American hours."

Do you miss friends and family? Make yourself get out and get involved. Meet new friends. Or do as one of our respondents did:

I was so lonely for my family and friends that I was miserable. So I wrote everyone back home great glowing letters of our new homeland and life style and invited virtually everybody, including distant cousins and college chums, to come and visit. To my surprise almost everyone accepted my offer, and I was so exhausted from playing tour guide and hostess that I had no time for loneliness.

Do you miss modern conveniences? Learn to improvise:

Candle-lit dinners had been so much the norm in our host country that when we returned to the States the children couldn't understand why we had electric lights instead of candles at night.

Are you dissatisfied with the education your children are receiving abroad? Consider one respondent's solution: every summer while on home leave, she enrolled her children in a tutoring program. These are but a few examples. As many expatriate wives have learned, it is best to attack your problems one at a time. Determine what situations can be changed and go at them with reasonable expectations.

Be flexible. If one problem-solving method doesn't seem to work, move on to another and another until the solution is found. If a situation is unchangeable, look for ways to make it more bearable. As one of the women interviewed said:

When we moved to the Far East, I left behind not only friends but my parents and all of my children, even my grandchild; and my husband traveled almost constantly. I determined to make the best of it. I became involved in everything that interested me culturally, socially, and philanthropically. My success became apparent when I realized I no longer noticed the days passing and my husband questioned when I would find some time for him on the days he was at home.

There are also many ways of alleviating your general feelings of anxiety, such as exercise, behavioral reversal ("I will be positive, I will get up, get out, and get involved"), and assertiveness training. You might even pick up one of the many self-psyching books or tapes that are now available to give you more ideas.

You'll probably find many aspects of your new culture to be novel and stimulating. Once you conquer your culture shock the first time, you'll look forward to moving to other countries and experiencing more new cultures.

CHAPTER XII

Getting Around

METHODS AND CHOICES OF TRANSPORTATION ABROAD are not significantly different from those in the States. Most of the women we interviewed who lived in major cities—London, Paris, Madrid, Athens, Rome, Mexico City, and Hong Kong—found that their day-to-day tasks could be readily accomplished by walking or using public transportation and taxis. Private automobiles, they felt, were for the most part unnecessary. Families who lived outside of major cities were much more likely to have their own cars.

A word to the wise: make sure you carry a map with you at all times until you are completely familiar with your new surroundings. Although they are well meaning, strangers will often give you misleading directions, or you may misinterpret what you hear. A local map is indispensable.

Public Transportation

Good, low cost public transportation is available in the cities of most nations. In cities such as Paris, London, and Moscow, public transportation is excellent. As is the case in most U.S. cities, you will be able to tell whether your new host country's public transportation is suitable for you and your family by doing two things: look for yourself—if the trains and buses are really overcrowded and dirty, you should probably think about carpooling with some of your neighbors or using taxicabs; find out what your peers do—you should probably do the same.

Driving

In many countries you will be allowed to drive a car if you possess a valid driver's license. Other countries require an international driving permit, which should be obtained, before you move, from an AAA office. Some countries, such as the United Kingdom, will require you to obtain a local driver's license by taking an extensive examination. Other countries will allow you to obtain a local license without taking an examination; some countries require no license at all.

Having determined the criteria for driving in your host country, there will be little left for you to do except to adjust to the local driving conditions and learn your way around. In some developing countries, this can be a humorous and sometimes harrowing experience:

In the U.S., cars will remain in single or double file at traffic lights. Not so in some parts of Latin America. Drivers scramble for advantageous starting positions. They fan out into as many lanes as possible while waiting for the green light; they even create new lanes! When the light changes, each driver thinks "me first" and the fastest car wins.

In some European countries, driving provides lessons in assertiveness:

> It was not long before I became used to the aggressive driving that is normal in European cities. Americans wait for an opening before they cross intersections, but that ties things up. The trick is to GO. European drivers tend to be very alert and they will take their feet off the accelerators for a few seconds, allowing you just enough time to get by.

In such countries as England, Australia, former British colonies, and parts of Africa, it will all be quite familiar except that you have to learn to keep to the left instead of the right. But once you learn to drive "on the wrong side of the road," you shouldn't have any other problems.

Shopping

As is the case in the States, shopping around the world involves a variety of stores and a variety of goods to be bought. Some of the world's finest supermarkets can be found in Saudi Arabia, and the boutiques of some of the world's best clothing designers can be found in Mexico City. No matter where you and your family are posted, finding out what is available in your area is bound to be both a treat and a challenge.

If you find that there are no supermarkets in your area, you will probably also find that there are more than enough individual vendors and marketplaces to meet your needs. If you cannot find a department or clothing store, you will surely be able to find fabric shops, tailors, and shops that sell beautiful locally made clothes. Far Eastern fabrics are exquisite, and tailors or seamstresses are cheap by American standards. Hand-embroidered Mexican and Latin American clothes are luxury items in the States but are extremely reasonably priced when sold in their countries of origin. Do not pass up the opportunities you will have to buy local handicrafts and artifacts that you would not be able to buy at home; you will never regret those purchases.

Again, as is the case in the States, supermarkets and department stores all over the world have fixed prices and fixed methods of payment. Major credit cards are accepted in almost all major city stores, as are travelers checks. In the smaller shops and markets of some countries the use of cash may be a possible source of discount, and paying in U.S. dollars may also bring you a better price on some purchases, especially in countries where hard currency is in demand.

CHAPTER XIII

Day-to-Day Etiquette

W E TAKE IT FOR GRANTED THAT EVERYONE KNOWS the basics of etiquette. However, every country is different and every country's customs are different. As an expatriate, you are a guest in the host country and you should behave as such.

The Basics

At some time during your sojourn abroad you will probably have to deal with anti-American criticism. No matter how unfair that criticism may seem to you, do not become visibly angry or abusive. To do so would only reinforce the critic's impression that Americans are undesirables. Many veteran expatriates have suggested that, when faced with criticism, try to diffuse the tension by admitting that from some points of view the criticism might be justified but from others it might not. In other words, draw the critic into a rational discussion of the problem and possible solutions for it. Whatever you do, save your display of anger for a moment when you are not in public.

You will also be faced with a constant question: "How do you like my country?" There will always be something pleasant to say by way of an answer. Do your best to be complimentary even if you would much rather be critical. Avoid the subjects of politics and religion. Some countries have laws mandating instant deportation if foreigners are heard to criticize the local government. As you may or may not know, some countries don't even bother with deportation: they simply jail you for the offense. The best way to get along in your host country is to find out what the "touchy" subjects are and then avoid them. There will be plenty of other things to talk about.

Tipping

Tipping customs vary from area to area. In parts of western Europe tips are considered demeaning by the recipients because they perceive their jobs to be the performance of services for which they are automatically compensated. Often the tip amount is set by law and included in the bill. In many parts of Latin America and the Middle East, on the other hand, you will be expected to tip any person who does anything for you—the gasoline station attendant, the taxi driver, the postman, anyone at all. It is also very important to tip your servants whenever there are holidays.

Entertaining

Entertaining and being entertained in a foreign land are fascinating experiences. Naturally, there are many do's and don'ts that vary from country to country and from subculture to subculture within each country. If you want to be a successful hostess and guest in your host country, you will need to research the country's customs. Some of the topics you will need to explore include, but are not limited to: introductions, invitations, arrival and departure timing, smoking, drinking toasts, and table manners. Your new expatriate friends should be a valuable source of information on the finer points of local social etiquette. If your company has hired a consultant to train you and other prospective expatriates, be ready to ask a lot of questions:

—What are the customary ways of introducing someone or of being introduced?

—Are there customs as to who shall speak first, sit first, eat first, get up from the table first?

—Should invitations be made by letter, by telephone or in person?

—If an invitation is accepted, does that mean that the person will actually come?

—Is the invitee likely to bring other people along to the party?

—How punctual are guests expected to be?

—How late do guests usually stay? Is there a polite way of getting them to leave?

—Are there customary ways of eating?

—Are there customary ways of sitting at the dining table? For instance, is it all right to put one or both elbows or wrists on the table?

—Is it expected that host and guest alike will make toasts throughout the meal? Are there rules about the toasts, their content, their length?

—When and where is it acceptable to smoke?

—When and where is it acceptable to drink alcohol?

Social Faux Pas

You will inevitably commit a social faux pas at some point during your stay abroad; we all do. U.S. nationals often laugh things off, whereas nationals of other countries often consider laughter a sign of disrespect in the wake of an impropriety. Therefore, a blunder may be followed by silence and averted eyes. Unfortunately, such a reaction may make a newcomer feel even more awkward. Never mind, since the best way to learn is by making mistakes, don't take the silence or the laughter to heart. If you think you have blundered, ask a friend to explain what you did wrong and rest assured that you will be forgiven, especially if you acknowledge your mistake, as this woman did:

> Shortly after we moved to London we attended a formal business dinner for about five hundred people affiliated with my husband's industry. After the first course had been completed, I lit a cigarette as I waited for the next course to be served. I didn't notice that I was the only smoker until the coffee was served, when the host/master of ceremonies rose from his place at the head table and announced: "You have the Queen's permission to smoke," at which point the majority of the crowd lit up. This was one English tradition I learned the hard way.

Just to prove the point that *everyone* makes mistakes, we include the following man's story:

> It was my first week in Tunisia. After a formal dinner, we were served half-full cups of coffee as thick as mud. I assumed that the accompanying glass of water was there for each guest to dilute his coffee to taste. But after I'd diluted mine I realized to my hor-

ror that the other guests were using the water to rinse their mouths in preparation for what turned out to be an almost sacred ritual of drinking the strong, dense brew.

I blushed from embarrassment for the first time in twenty years, but the other men at the table pretended that they hadn't noticed that anything was wrong. From that time on I learned to watch before doing anything I was unfamiliar with doing.

One of our interviewees provided us with a very useful piece of advice: when you are new to a country, take time at the end of each day to talk with the other members of your family about your experiences that day. Even your children will have tales to tell and lessons to teach. You are also likely to find these etiquette sessions quite amusing.

CHAPTER XIV

Cross-Cultural Communication

WHEN THINKING OF CROSS-CULTURAL COMMUNICATION, we sometimes mistakenly think only of language. True cross-cultural communication, however, involves both nonverbal and verbal communication.

Why Is Nonverbal Communication Important?

You communicate through your gestures, facial expressions, posture, mode of walking, eye contact, and direction of gaze. Your clothes, jewelry, hair style, and make-up also send continuous nonverbal signals. Through intended and unintended means, you constantly indicate your feelings, attitudes, beliefs, and values. Pay as much attention to your nonverbal signals as you pay to language and you can avoid some unpleasant and embarrassing situations.

I was never so embarrassed in all of life! There I was, having what I thought was a polite conversation with the wife of a Latin American diplomat, gesturing obscenities the whole time! What I didn't know was the fact that the OK sign—forming a circle with my thumb and index finger while raising the other three fingers—is a very grave insult, an obscenity, in many Latin American countries.

If, before you relocate, you can talk with someone familiar with local customs, that person may be able to give you tips on what not to do. However, even if you are lucky enough to be forewarned, there may still be anxiety-provoking situations you didn't anticipate. Rest assured, most people are able to recognize gestures and expressions used in ignorance and will not take offense. If they laugh, laugh with them and ask what you did wrong. They will probably respect you all the more for your ability to laugh at yourself, and they will probably be pleased and proud to teach you about their cultural mannerisms.

What About Verbal Communication?

The ability to speak the host country language can make your assignment abroad more successful and enjoyable. Your ability to say what you want when you want and to understand what is said to you will give you self-confidence and a greater degree of comfort while you live abroad. Also, the ability to speak even a few words and phrases in the local langauge is greatly appreciated by the local nationals—they see that ability as evidence that you have a positive attitude about the country and its people. Put yourself in their place, and think of how you'd feel meeting someone who hadn't bothered to learn a little English even though he or she was residing in the States.

Culture and language studies go hand in hand, and we must assume that if you weren't a little bit interested in learning about other cultures you would not have agreed to move. The extent to which you do learn the language of your host country is directly related to the amount you can learn about its culture and heritage.

Another heartening fact is that bilingualism may be economically beneficial. You may, because of your language skills, have opened up new avenues by being a more attractive applicant for high-level jobs at home and abroad—jobs for which you might never otherwise have applied.

How Can You Learn the Language?

There are many ways to learn the language. Of course, getting a head start before you move would be ideal; but few prospective expatriates have the time to take language lessons while they are preparing for their outward-bound trip. Once you've moved, however, individual teachers can be found in most communities—you will probably be able to choose between "total immersion" courses, four-week, six-week, semester, and year-long courses.

If you find your new schedule to be erratic, a private tutor might prove the best method. Or you can enroll in a local bilingual/bicultural university or college. Surprisingly, U.S.-sponsored overseas university programs are conducted in most major cities of the world. Self-taught home study courses are also available. Using tape-recorded lessons and accompanying textbooks, you can set your own pace. Some people even create their own "total immersion" programs by spending their time conversing with their neighbors, local merchants, and household help and by watching local television.

Regardless of which method you choose, you will probably find that you will absorb much of the language painlessly as you go about your daily tasks in the new host country.

Will You Ever Become Fluent?

The truth is, few people who live abroad for only two or three years become totally fluent in the host country language. By the end of such period, most expatriates are able to read, write, speak, and understand a lot of the language, but few are able to think and react as a native.

There are also degrees of fluency, and your progress will depend on your motivation and goals. At the earliest possible time, decide realistically what level of fluency you wish to reach and by when.

Choose your method of reaching it, and then implement your plan. As is the case with most projects, the first step—be it enrolling in a course or approaching the local news vendor for a conversation—is the hardest step to take. Don't procrastinate. Many of the women we interviewed said that once they reached their goals they set new ones and surprised themselves by far surpassing their original expectations.

Some of our interviewees' language goals will give you a good idea of the range of your options. Almost everyone wanted to learn the basic daily-need and courtesy phrases and to be able to converse in social settings. Most also wanted to be able to learn enough to be able to give clear orders to their servants and have their homes run smoothly. Some said they wanted to learn enough to enjoy watching local television and feel free to travel alone. Just a few wanted to achieve total fluency.

What If You Think You Can't Learn Another Language?

Attitude is a crucial factor in whether you learn the language of a new country—not only your attitude about your capacity for learning, but also your beliefs about the language to be learned. If you are having difficulty, ask yourself the following questions:

—Do you like and accept your new environment, and are you comfortable with the nationals?
—Do you believe that Americans can't learn another language as easily as people from other countries?
—Do you dislike your method of instruction?
—Do you consider learning the language a waste of time because you can't foresee using the language other than while residing in the host country?
—Do you feel inferior when you try to speak the language?
—Are you too shy?
—Are you afraid you might fail?

If this list of questions contains your personal reason(s) for not learning the host country language, take heart. Other expatriates share your fears and feelings. The fact is, everyone can learn a few basic phrases just by hearing them on a daily basis. Once you've realized that you've picked up some of the language without even trying, you should find it easier to set further, realistic language goals and to work toward achieving them.

I first learned the words and phrases I needed to train the maid and get the house in order from a friend who was fluent in the language. Then I started on the vocabulary for the daily shopping and some of the common social phrases.

When I felt a sense of organization at home, I signed up for basic-beginners language lessons at the Newcomers Club. I've always been terrible at learning languages, and I avoided them all through school. But the lessons have made me feel comfortable with my basic knowledge. I'll never be fluent, but I can get through any emergency. Sure, some of my neighbors speak the language better than I do. That's all right. I've chosen to spend my time learning to do other things.

* * *

I didn't try to learn the language. I couldn't even read it, as it was nonphonetic. I did master reading the numbers for shopping and tried to pick up some vocabulary. I was totally surprised, after a year, to realize I'd picked up a 600-word vocabulary!

If you are a person who learns languages easily, you are rare and will probably avoid some of the frustrations and pitfalls that the rest of us experience. Learning a language takes time. If you apply yourself to the task every day, at home and in classes, you will learn just as much as you wish to.

CHAPTER XV

Day-to-Day
Resources

ONCE YOU HAVE THE HOUSING AND SCHOOL situation in hand, your next priority will be to learn to function in your new homeland as if you were *not* a foreigner. Besides learning some of the language, your daily routine will require you to know how to handle the local currency and banking methods, the local transit system, phone system, and the services necessary for your family's needs. You will probably need to learn the metric system of measurements; and you will certainly have to learn all of the elements of local business and social etiquette. Some of these tasks will be easier than others. Don't be bashful. Get on with it. You will find many people in your new environment eager to assist you and many others traveling the same path. Lasting friendships almost always develop among people who share, cry, and laugh over the tribulations of "settling-in."

Your Embassy

American embassies abroad fulfill a dual function. Primarily, they represent the U.S. government on foreign soil. Secondarily, but of more interest to Americans abroad, embassies provide consular services. The function of the embassy's consular section is to assist, "to a limited extent," Americans traveling and residing in the host country. The reason for saying "limited" is that the embassy can only assist to the extent that is "legally consistent" with the laws of the host country. Embassy staff members, like you, must obey those laws. Consequently, it is important that you keep in mind that what is legal in the States may not be legal in your host country.

The U.S. State Department provides informative pamphlets to U.S. travelers, such as "Your Trip Abroad" and "Know Before You Go," which generally cover the subjects of taxation and customs regulations. The State Department will also provide pamphlets about particular areas and corresponding laws and restrictions. To obtain State Department publications, write to: U.S. Department of State, Washington, DC 20044.

Also, if you have time to visit the host country before you move, try to stop by the embassy. Speak to staff members and have them explain the services that are available at that particular embassy. Once you have moved to your new country, there may be some time before your household belongings arrive, and so this, too, is an excellent time to visit the embassy.

It would be impossible to list all the services that embassies can provide. We will mention the key services, however, which are likely to be available. The embassy may be able to provide you with lists of translators, English-speaking qualified dentists and doctors, American schools, American banks, and English-speaking attorneys. The embassy can renew your passport or issue one for your newborn child. The embassy staff will also be able to help you obtain copies of host country public records, such as birth, marriage, and death certificates. The embassy staff may also be available to steer you through the morass of local laws and paperwork connected with these events. Should you be arrested, a representative of the embassy will visit you immediately after being notified of your arrest to make sure that your legal rights are upheld (within the framework of *that* country's laws). The representative will provide you with names of attorneys, inform your family if you so desire, and lodge protests in the event that you are mistreated. The embassy will also assist you when it comes time to vote, register with the Selective Service, have documents notarized, or file your taxes. Most embassy staffs include representatives of particular federal agencies, such as Social Security, Internal Revenue Service, Veterans Administration, and Civil Service, to name but a few.

Embassies are not identical. Consular service sections are flexible and designed to meet the needs of U.S. citizens in each particular country, given local conditions. Familiarize yourself with your embassy's services, and let the staff know your needs; in turn, the staff will be better able to serve you and the rest of the expatriate community.

Currency

Try to learn what the local currency is prior to your departure. If possible, obtain some of the currency in various denominations so you can learn to recognize the sizes, types, and values of coins, as well as sizes, colors, and values of bills. Practice until you can immediately recognize the money for what it is. Learn the conversion formulas by heart. You don't really want to give a hundred dollar tip to the grocery boy instead of one dollar. You'll be surprised how quickly you'll learn to think in your new local currency. Until then, if you're not handy with figures, carry a pocket calculator or conversion chart for reference.

Banking

It is advisable to open a bank account in the "new" country before you arrive. It is not uncommon to encounter a waiting period between the time you open the account and the time you can actually withdraw funds. Many expatriates advise using a major multinational bank with overseas branches, taking advantage of its ability to exchange currencies, transfer funds, continue your credit standing, and allow you to take care of your financial matters wherever the bank has an office.

You should also be aware of the Bank Secrecy Act, which requires you to report amounts exceeding $5,000 U.S. dollars brought in or out of the States. According to this law you must report any foreign bank accounts when filing your income tax. The same law requires that all U.S. banks and other financial institutions report all transactions and remittances made to any individual outside the States involving more than $10,000.

Mail

In many countries you may find it best to have your mail addressed to your office or to a post office box. Offices tend to have more frequent and regular mail deliveries, including magazine and parcel deliveries. In some countries, since the mail is not regularly delivered to individual homes, magazines and packages have to be collected by the addressee.

To hasten international mail, keep stamps on hand; and when friends travel to the States, ask them if they would mail your letters and bill payments. *Never request that a person carry a wrapped package for you.* As customs will undoubtedly open the package, we advise you to put the item in a box that can easily be opened and closed. Although you may be a trusting individual, do not, under any circumstances, carry wrapped packages for anyone else. Innocent and generous people have ended up being innocent victims and carriers of contraband because they wanted to do a friend a favor. If you carry an unwrapped package for someone else, make sure that person provides you with documents that identify the package's contents and value.

Before you send money orders or personal checks through the mail, make sure that doing so is legal. It may be illegal for money in any form to be sent or taken out of the country. In some countries, mail is inspected and your check could be appropriated. You also risk the possibility of the check being lost or stolen.

Telephones

Telephone systems abroad are not the same as those of the States. You will probably find that the variety of telephone and telephone services found in the States is not available abroad. If you are assigned to a post in a developing nation, try to find a house or apartment with working telephone service. If you can't have a phone, improvise.

We were living in a new apartment building in a Middle Eastern country. The place was wonderful, but for one thing—there was no phone. We had been assured by numerous officials that "it was only a matter of time until telephone lines will be put into the area and you are at the top of the list to get one." Fortunately, there was another American family in the building who fully understood our predicament and allowed us to use their phone when we needed it.

One night, as we all discussed the lack of progress on the part of the phone company, we hit on a temporary solution: we would use an extension phone that would connect our apartments! At first we thought we'd have to run a long cord out one window, down six floors, and in another window. But we discovered that extending the phone would be even easier than that: our landlord had all the apartments wired for phones and there was a main terminal in the basement; all we had to do was connect two wires in the terminal box.

This party line continued for almost two years. We were transferred to another country before we got our own phone line. But, you know, our solution proved to be a great arrangement for all of us. We took messages, gave messages, and forwarded phone calls for each other. I even ended up rushing my neighbor's child to the hospital one day because I was at home and she wasn't when the school called to say there was an emergency.

You must accept that, wherever you are posted, your new host country's telephone system will be idiosyncratic—you may be faced with odd dialing techniques, frequent disconnections, crossed lines, and no service during rainstorms. Expatriates who live with such complications learn to say what they have to say quickly and concisely. Our own experiences and those of our interviewees have also led us to make the following recommendation: if allowed, bring a phone with an automatic redial button. It helps when you are trying to make an international call and have to dial numerous times to catch a free line.

Metrics

There are only a handful of countries that do not measure by the kilometer, liter, and gram. Unfortunately, the United States is one of them. Preferably before you move, but at least before you go shopping, make sure you have a pamphlet or chart that explains the metric system. Metrics are not difficult to master; and, like the basics of conversation in the host country language, after a short period of living with the metric system you will find yourself thinking in kilos and meters rather than pounds and inches.

CHAPTER XVI

Servants

NOT ALL EXPATRIATE FAMILIES HAVE SERVANTS, but it is a common aspect of overseas living. Of the women we interviewed, virtually all who chose not to hire a servant either had no children at home or lived in a country where wages were high. The choice will be yours.

If you decide to hire a servant, you will inevitably hear comments from stateside friends like:

> What a luxury! You don't have to worry about washing the dishes or doing the laundry. Instead, you have all the free time you want during the day! I envy you.

*   *   *

> Everyone who lives overseas lives better because they have servants, and for such a pittance. I'd give anything to have someone around the house all day to take care of the children.

To an outsider, having a maid—let alone a chauffeur, gardener, laundress, or cook—is sheer luxury. A household servant can indeed be a blessing. However, having a servant does not mean that you will have unlimited free time. As an employer, you will have to make the decisions, give the orders, and monitor and be responsible for everything that goes on in your house. Having a servant is work and can, in fact, be a source of real frustration for family members. If you tap your local grapevine before moving abroad, you may find that "servant stories" rival "moving stories" in quantity and detail. *Do not be put off!* With patience, understanding, and work you will be able to find, train, and keep the kind of servant who is a blessing while you are overseas.

Should You Hire Household Help?

There are a multitude of reasons for hiring household help. We found, especially when expatriate families include children, that the greater the difference between the new host country and the States in terms of language, culture, and climate, the greater the need for household help.

In many countries—especially those in Latin America, the Middle East, and the Far East—it is traditional for members of the "upper" and "middle" classes to have servants. All countries have class systems, though some refuse to admit it. Although you may think of yourself as "middle" class in the States, you may find that your new host country has no "middle" class. As an American expatriate—no matter where you are living and no matter what your financial, company, or social position may be in reality—you will be regarded by others as a member of the "upper" class. If you are transferred to a country in which, as an expatriate, you will be expected to hire at least one servant, you will find the assimilation process much easier if you follow this custom.

Many American women, especially, if they are used to doing everything themselves and are proud of it, find it difficult to have servants in the beginning. For example, one of the wives we interviewed stated that she had resolved to live without a servant. However, after living in her new home for a very short time, she changed her mind:

Since I knew that we would be living outside the States for only two years, I decided that I did not want to disrupt my family's pattern of each member being responsible for certain household chores. The first time that I got an inkling that I had made an error in judgment was when I went to put the garbage out.

I had been told that every few days a man would walk down the street ringing a bell, at which point a person from every house would bring the trash out to the truck, which would be following on the heels of the bell ringer. So, dressed in jeans and a tee-shirt, I lugged my trash to the street. In that instant I realized that I could not make this part of my routine.

All along the street were clusters of maids in uniform, standing with their respective bundles. I knew from the looks on their faces that it was most peculiar for the lady of the house to attend to this chore.

Just as I was about to retreat, the garbage truck pulled up in front of me. The garbagemen jumped down and relieved me of my bundles. When I looked down the street again, to my dismay, not only were the maids staring at me, but some of my new neighbors were as well. I quickly retreated to my home.

Later that afternoon, a neighborhood "representative" came over and explained to me the who, why, and how of the proper method of garbage disposal. Since it was apparent that I would invite the wrath of my neighbors and would incite their servants to dis-

content if I did not hire a maid, I set about the task of
hiring one.

Servants can and do become annoyed when they see
expatriate wives performing tasks which servants feel are
theirs to do. And "upper" class women become annoyed
when they see their peers working at tasks which are perceived to be the servants' duties. Also, many expatriates
believe that hiring a servant can be an important contribution to the economy of the host country.

Security is also a prime motivation for hiring household help. In some countries it is desirable to have someone in your house at all times. This is a fact of life—just as
it is a fact of life in New York City, for example, that you
need to have extra locks on your front door. The extra
locks do not, however, make New York City any less of a
business, educational, or cultural treasure trove. If you are
transferred to an area where security is an issue, hire a
servant and go about your business as usual.

There are many other good reasons for hiring servants—either live-in or daily. You may be lucky enough to
live in a country where American women can get working
papers, and you may, therefore, choose to work outside of
your home all day. You may want someone to help out
who can speak English as well as the native language. You
may live in an area where individual vendors will come
to your door throughout the day, and you may want someone to answer the door and make the purchases while you
take care of other tasks. Or you may live in a country
where foods can only be purchased in their natural states
and where shopping for dinner—let alone preparing it—
takes up most of the day. In such a situation, you'd never
get anything done if you didn't have help.

No matter what stateside people say or think, you will
probably find that servants are often an absolute necessity
and rarely a luxury. If you think you need a servant, figure

out why and then find someone who will fulfill your
needs or train someone to do so.

What Types of Servants Do Most Expatriates Employ?

The size and location of your new housing, your budget, your spouse's position and responsibilities, the degree to which you will be working outside your home,
and the number of children in your family are major factors to consider in determining the number and type of
servants you may want to employ.

You may also find that you have been transferred to an
area where it is next to impossible to find servants who
will perform more than one task. However, when possible, hire someone who can perform two or three tasks.
Such a servant's salary will typically be less than what
you would pay two or three different servants, each of
whom would perform only one task. You will not only
save money on food, uniforms, and expenses but also
avoid possible personality conflicts.

The following list includes the most common types of
servants hired by expatriates around the world: daily or
live-in maid, cook, driver, bearer, bodyguard, nursemaid,
governess, laundress, houseboy, butler, valet, seamstress/
tailor, window washer, and gardener.

You will find that the daily or live-in maid is by far the
most common type of servant employed by your fellow
expatriates, no matter where you live.

Should the Company Be Responsible?

No. That is, no more than the company would be financially responsible for your household employees in the

States. If the company requires you to entertain for business reasons, it may be amenable to contributing to such entertainment costs, including wages. Otherwise, the only example of company involvement that we know of are instances in which companies provide chauffeurs and/or bodyguards for their employees. Chauffeurs or bodyguards are not simply perks of office. More often than not, traffic conditions, the need for efficient use of time, the employee's personal security, and the business/social stature of the company necessitate the hiring of such a person.

How Do You Find a Servant?

One of the best and most reliable ways to find a servant is through a friend or fellow expatriate. You will probably discover that one of your new neighbors has a servant who has a relative or friend who is looking for a job. American or women's club newsletters or bulletin boards are another source for finding help. There are also agencies that handle domestic help in most cities throughout the world. Before you use an agency, however, ask around to make sure that it is reputable and that its fees are reasonable. You could also place an advertisement in the local English-language newspaper or radio. If you choose this route, give your phone number only and try to arrange initial interviews with applicants outside your home.

There are servants who attempt to find employment by going from door to door in search of a job. Most of these people have no credentials and no references, but they do have the need for, and desire to, work. Use your judgment. There are never any guarantees, no matter what method is used to find an employee, that the person hired will turn out to be right for you.

What About Wages?

There is no way to predetermine how much your servant's wages should be. Costs vary from country to country and from year to year, depending on the supply and demand for servants and on the value of the dollar relative to the host country currency.

The best way to ascertain the going rate is to ask other expatriates what they pay. If you can, for perspective, ask local national friends who have servants what they pay. You can assume, no matter where you live abroad, that Americans often pay more for servants than the local nationals do. There are good reasons for this, one of which is that Americans tend to want servants who can speak English. This ability commands a premium price. Other factors include whether your household help lives in your home or comes on a daily basis and whether your servant will be expected to perform more than one job.

How Should Interviews With Prospective Servants Be Handled?

If you do not speak the native language, find a friend or neighbor who can translate for you temporarily. If you know that you will be needing more than one servant, try to interview and hire someone who is bilingual and will be responsible for managing the other servants and who can, therefore, take part in the interviewing process.

Before conducting the interview(s), talk to your neighbors and find out what tasks are normally given to particular servants. Decide which tasks you wish to handle yourself and which you wish the servant(s) to do. During the interview, make sure that the following subjects are covered and that your expectations and those of your prospective employee(s) are absolutely understood: prior work experiences and references; job definition; daily, weekly, monthly work schedule; days off, vacations; rest periods; meals; rules for visitors to the employee(s); health requirements; personal hygiene requirements; wearing and provision of uniforms; general appearance; salary, raises, bonuses, social security system equivalents; government requirements: registration and/or bonding.

Customs regarding these subjects vary from country to country. Try to familiarize yourself with your host country's customs by speaking with your local and expatriate neighbors before conducting any interviews.

Who's the Boss?

This may seem to be a strange question—who's the boss? Obviously, you are! Pretty elementary, you might say. Unfortunately, there are many countries—especially those in the Middle East—where neither the question nor the answer is elementary. In countries where women are thought to be inferior to men, you must make sure that your household help—female and male alike—understands from the very beginning that *you are the boss*. If you neglect to make this clear at the outset, you may find yourself powerless in your own home. Even if you have to, ask your husband to tell the servants that you will be giving the orders, address the issue as soon as possible.

When we moved to the Middle East, one of the first servants we hired was a chauffeur/handyman. My husband had to go on a business trip two days after we moved into the new house, so I was left with the task of putting everything in order.

In the process of getting things done, I asked the chauffeur to deliver payment for and bring back the drapery fabric I had ordered. He was astounded that I was making a major decision without consulting my husband and respectfully suggested that we wait "until Master comes home to give his approval." I told him there was no need for the "master's" approval, as I usually handled such matters. To my surprise, he then suggested that we obtain the approval of my son—who was four and a half years old at the time! Our chauffeur explained that, in the absence of the husband, the oldest son is considered head of the household. I, in turn, explained how our household was managed. Though doubtful, the chauffeur did as I asked. When my husband returned from his business trip, he assured our chauffeur that I was indeed the boss in our home. After that, we and our chauffeur had many good years together.

How Do You Manage Your Servants?

Most American women are not accustomed to having household help and, because they are used to doing everything themselves, find giving orders to other adults difficult at first. Here are some tips culled from our interviews with other expatriate wives:

Learn at least enough of the native language to communicate the day-to-day business of your home simply and clearly.

Make sure that your tasks and those of your servant(s) are clearly understood.

More than simply defining the servant's job, state what the objectives are and give standards by which the both of you will be able to evaluate performance. *Do not change your expectations or your standards.*

Because time does not have the same meaning for everyone, make sure that time patterns are established which are mutually acceptable: How much time will be allowed for the completion of each task? How much leisure time will the servant(s) have each day?

Treat your servant as you would want to be treated if you were in his or her place: *Be firm, be fair, be consistent.* Be a good employer.

Should There Be a Probation Period?

Although interviews can be revealing, there is no better way than arranging for a probation period to find out whether a particular servant will suit you and your family.

It is extremely important that you use the probation period to train your prospective employee. Servants are not mind readers. Without clear training, there is no way that a servant will measure up to your expectations. Make sure that the person in question knows why there should be such a period, how much he or she is to be paid during that time, and that your final decision will be made at the end of it.

The length of the probation period should depend on the job—it should be longer if the servant is to be responsible for a number of tasks. The usual range is from one week to one month. Also, most expatriate employers raise their servants' salaries as soon as the servants become official members of the household.

What Are Your Responsibilities as an Employer?

Once again, your responsibilities, including legal responsibilities, will vary from country to country. The best way to find out what is customary in your new area is to talk with a local national, someone at the nearest U.S. em-

bassy, or a lawyer. Some of the questions you should ask
are:

- —Are you required to register the employee with a local
  government agency?
- —Are you required to pay social security or other types
  of taxes for the employee?
- —Are you required to pay for the employee's health
  care? If so, is there a ceiling on how much you will be
  liable for during any given year?
- —How many paid and unpaid holidays is an employee
  entitled to?
- —How much paid vacation is an employee entitled to?
- —Are female employees entitled to paid maternity
  leave? If so, what is the usual length of time allowed
  for such a leave of absence?
- —To what extent will you be liable if one of your employees breaks a local law?
- —Do you need liability insurance?
- —Are you required to provide severance pay if you fire
  an employee for any reason? Are there any exceptions? What if the employee leaves of his or her own
  volition?
- —If one of your employees dies while under contract to
  you, will you be liable for funeral expenses?
- —Are you required to provide clothing for your employees? If so, how much and of what type?

Should You Have a Written Contract?

Some country's laws require written contracts between
employers and servants; such contracts are strictly optional in other countries. Contracts do have advantages
for both the employer and the employee, one of the great-

est being a guarantee that works both ways: for X amount of services the employee will receive Y amount of pay. We recommend that you use contracts with your employees; it's good business. Make sure that your contract includes a very clear description of the employee's job.

Whether you choose to use a written contract, be zealous in keeping accurate and up-to-date records of your servant's salary, bonuses, holidays, vacations, and termination circumstances, if there are any. It is not unheard of for servants to sue their former employers, whether or not there was a written contract and regardless of the reasons for termination. Many of the expatriates we spoke to suggested that servants be required to sign receipts when receiving their salaries and bonuses. Our sources also strongly recommended that when a servant leaves your employ, he or she should sign a statement attesting to full payment as of that date including severance pay and, when appropriate, that he or she is leaving of his or her own volition.

If you are sued for any reason, consider another piece of advice: settle the matter out of court. You may feel that you are being wronged and have a good case, but it will end up costing a lot less to settle and have done with it.

What Child Care Responsibilities Should You Give a Servant?

Obviously the answer depends on the servant and what sort of child care experience he or she has had. Make sure that anyone you hire to take care of your children has good references. Check the references thoroughly, making sure that the servant's training and experience will suit the respective ages of your children.

Try to spend a lot of time training the servant to care for your children as you would. Once again, *without clear instructions, the servant will not be able to live up to your expectations.*

We also have a word or two of caution about maids and American children. Most children who are raised in the States are accustomed to picking up and putting away their belongings and helping with chores around the house. When there's a maid around whose job is to keep everything neat and tidy, children can become very lazy and careless. Children can also develop "bossy" attitudes if no one intervenes. Treat yourself, as well as your servants and your children, right: make sure that your children continue to be responsible for certain tasks wherever you live and no matter how big your household staff may be. Make sure, also, that your children understand that servants are people too and that respect is due to all people.

If you have chosen not to employ a servant and you have children you will obviously need a babysitter every now and then. If you are posted to a city, such as London or Paris, you will probably discover the existence of nanny services that can provide sitters by the day, hour, and week. Most of these services are reliable and most of their employees are well trained, but it is always best to check before hiring. There are other sources of babysitters, such as schools and universities, women's clubs, churches, and local boy and girl scout groups.

What Kinds of Problems Are Common When You Have Household Employees?

The problems which can arise with servants are limitless. Some of the most common are as follows: difficulty with or lack of communication, conflicts between servants, servant's family problems interfering with work, servant's expectation that you will help his or her relatives financially or to find work, servant entertaining friends in your home, servant trying on your clothing or jewelry, servant spending too much time on the telephone, chronic absenteeism or lateness, drunkenness (or drinking on the job), sexual promiscuity/pregnancy, severe illness, and lying/stealing.

Take some advice, and do your best to prevent problems from arising right from the beginning. You are the employer and it is your responsibility to make sure there is a clear understanding of what you will allow. Using the above list as a foundation, create a list of rules. Make sure the servant understands that these rules must be observed if he or she wishes to remain in your employment. If you use a written contract, include the rules.

If a Problem Does Arise, How Should You Handle It?

Handle any problem carefully and with patience. Talk to the servant about what you think happened. Listen to the servant's explanation, and make sure there has been no misunderstanding on either side. You might also want to talk with a fellow expatriate or a local national friend to make sure that the action and your reaction make sense.

We had a terrific maid who developed a back disorder and eventually could not do any heavy cleaning or bedmaking. We were attached to her, and she kept our home running smoothly; so we decided to hire a second maid to do the heavy work. Our first maid was willing to take a slight pay cut to help cover the expense of a second maid; she also took on the task of training her helper.

Do not fly off the handle and do something you may later regret, as this woman did:

> I dismissed my maid for thievery, only to find out later that my dog was the guilty party! He had buried all of my missing things in the garden.

Make sure that you have thought about how serious the problem really is and how sure you are that the servant was really responsible before you take any action. Do not take any action before you've heard the servant's side of the story.

How Do You Fire a Servant?

First, make sure you know the laws of your host country. Many countries have very restrictive laws concerning the employer-employee relationship. There may be legal statutes that expressly define causes for dismissal and circumstances under which the employer must give the former employee severance pay. No matter where you live, justified causes probably include the following: false references, dishonesty, violence, excessive absenteeism, drunkenness, or gross negligence.

If you find that you have to fire an employee, above all, be tactful. Try not to get angry. Try to defuse the situation and avoid further unpleasantness by being honest about your reasons for the termination of employment. Also, be fair about severance pay and letters of recommendation.

What If You Have to Terminate a Servant Because You Are Being Transferred?

As a rule, most expatriates are very good about giving their servants what is due them, plus extras. Many expatriates that we interviewed said that they always tried to go out of their way to make sure that their employees had new jobs before they were transferred. It should not be difficult to place a good servant; most of our sources said that they found this to be a pleasant and rewarding task.

How Do You Keep a Good Servant?

The obvious answer is: give regular raises, bonuses, and other incentives, such as Christmas and birthday gifts. Be tactful and respect your employee's pride. Make it seem as though the employee is doing you a favor by accepting your gifts.

All of our respondents told us that a major factor in getting and keeping good servants is attitude. *Be courteous, considerate, respectful, and pleasant, and make sure that all other family members do the same.*

Some of our interviews led us to this warning. There are people overseas who, like executive headhunters, will try to steal your best employees out from under your nose. *Do not boast about how good your maid is.* Word will get around, and someone will surely be tempted to lure her away. One of our respondents had this story to tell:

I was thrilled about our young housekeeper; she mastered every task so quickly. One afternoon a neighbor came to visit and mentioned how impressed she was with my new housekeeper. I fell for it and spent quite a long time extolling the young woman's virtues. When my neighbor carried her dish into the kitchen and lingered a while to converse with my housekeeper, it did not occur to me that my neighbor could be making a better offer to my house-keeper in the hope of stealing her away. And do you know what? My housekeeper left! After that I learned to contain my enthusiasm.

Keep the lines of communication open between you and your employees. Let them know that you are aware of their value. If you know that someone has approached your wonderful housekeeper, caution her about the pos-sibility of an offer looking better than it really is. Suggest that she discuss any offers with you to see if you can reach an acceptable compromise. Another respondent had this reassuring tale to tell:

When my maid was offered a higher monthly sal-ary to work for one of my neighbors, she came and told me about it and said that she was contemplating making the move. I wanted to keep her but could not afford to match the salary offered. When I asked a long-term resident about the woman who was taking my maid away, I learned that the woman had five screaming children and an exceptionally large house and was extremely demanding of her maids. So I de-cided to gamble.

I told my maid that I thought very highly of her and felt that she was certainly worth a higher salary but that I couldn't pay it. Therefore, I suggested that she go to work for the other woman on a trial basis, to see whether the job had some hidden disadvantages. I said that if she found that she wasn't happy in her new job I would welcome her back. She returned to us within a week and didn't even ask for an increase in pay. But I gave her a little something extra. I felt that otherwise it would have been awkward for her to explain to her friends why she returned.

Should You Try to Make a Servant Feel a Part of the Family?

If anything, try to make your servant feel part of the *team*. After all, you are probably not going to live in the host country for more than a few years. It wouldn't be fair to make the servant feel part of the family while you are there and then abandoned when you are gone. Only a few families will be able to, or will want to, take their servant with them when they move on or return home. We know of a number of families who employed servants long enough to develop family-like ties and who continued to send money and gifts to their former servants long after the families had moved. This is fine; but initially the relationship should be one of teamwork, not a seat at the dinner table.

CHAPTER XVII

Safeguarding Your Health and Home

As an expatriate wife, you probably will have many concerns about your family's medical care and security.

Medical Services

According to our survey, one of the most prevalent fears that exists for people living abroad is that they will be faced with inadequate medical services. For the most part, this fear is unjustified. You will probably be posted to a metropolitan area where you will be able to find plenty of local doctors and hospitals. If, however, you are posted to a less developed area, you may have difficulty in finding convenient medical services. However, there are usually prearranged transportation systems for medical emergencies, and as many of our respondents pointed out, the druggists of such less developed areas are used to providing treatment to the people who live nearby.

Preparation and organization is critical, no matter where you move. We have some suggestions:

—Make sure that every family member has a thorough checkup before you move, and arrange to have annual checkups when you return to the States for home leaves.

—Have all pertinent medical records translated into the local language, even if you are likely to be using an English-speaking doctor.

—Make sure that each family member carries medic alert identification detailing allergies and special health problems.

—Carry common medications used by your family and a small first aid kit. Be sure to date all medications.

—Carry extra sets of contact lenses or eyeglasses and a copy of all relevant prescriptions.

—Take a first aid course or a CPR course if you have time.

—Pack a medical reference book which will help you to recognize and treat common ailments, and explains dosages and side effects of medications.

Investigate emergency medical care facilities before any need arises. You may find that medical services must be paid for *in cash before they are performed* in your new host country. So it is extremely important that you take the time to visit the hospital nearest to your new home to find out about its emergency and admissions policies. If you discover that medical services will be provided on a cash-only and "up-front" basis at the hospital, you can assume that the same payment system will apply to other aspects of medical care, such as ambulance services and prescriptions. Take for example the experience of an executive's wife who was living in a sophisticated Middle Eastern city:

> I had injured my leg in a fall. As soon as the ambulance arrived, the attendants requested that I pay in advance for the trip to the hospital. I paid.
>
> When I arrived at the emergency room, I was told that I'd have to pay in advance for the use of the examining room and its personnel. I paid. I also paid, in advance, for the X-rays, antibiotic ointment, bandages, and pain-killers. Since the hospital wouldn't take a check and there was no such thing as credit, I was lucky I had cash in my purse.

Embassies usually provide lists of English-speaking physicians in the area, and your new neighbors will also be able to refer you to good local doctors. You can also obtain a list of qualified English-speaking doctors practicing in your host country by writing to: The International Association for Medical Assistance to Travelers, 736 Center Street, Lewiston, NY 14092.

Security

Security is also an important concern to expatriates. There are places where anti-American feelings run high, and where, as American corporate employees, you and your family may be prime kidnap targets. Aside from finding out what your company's security policy is and hiring a live-in servant to watch your house when you are not there, you might take the time to talk with a staff member at your local embassy about where and when you should look for potential trouble, as well as how to avoid it. You should also train yourself, your family, and your household staff to be aware and observant. Familiarize yourself with those who service your household, schools, and even your office. Try to learn to read their "body language" so that you will be able to sense when all is not right. Make an extra effort to keep abreast of current international and local affairs that might have an influence on your family.

There are two schools of thought on how best to secure your home and family. One is the high-profile method, which involves elaborate detection and alarm systems, guards, and other staff members. The other is the low-profile method, which mandates smaller homes, no limousines or flashy cars, and the same kind of household help that is employed by the local nationals.

We do not mean to alarm you or put you off. The fact of the matter is that in some countries, as in some U.S. cities, you must pay attention to your security. Only you and your family can determine what measures should be taken for your family's security.

PART FIVE

CHAPTER XVIII

You and the Corporation

WHEN IT COMES TO EXPATRIATE EMPLOYEES and their families, the importance of a company personnel department cannot be stressed too highly. Personnel departments—their impact and their capabilities—vary from company to company, depending on the authority vested in them by management and, more importantly, on the attitude, philosophy, and "hands-on" experience of the staff responsible for the company's expatriates.

In the course of our interviews we discovered that first-hand experience, or the lack of it, was the most critical attribute mentioned about anyone making decisions concerning expatriates and their families. Many of the interviewees commented that an experienced personnel director was to a great extent capable of compensating for any problems, lack of convenience, comfort, or benefits. It was clear that personnel directors who were sensitive to the costs, both psychological and monetary, of living and working abroad did much to tip the scales when expatri-

177

ate employees' families were determining whether their international experiences had been good ones and whether they should continue living and working as expatriates. To be born with such sensitivity is rare; it is usually obtained only through personal experience.

Expatriates are a flexible lot, but they are far more willing to accept the edicts of a person with experiences similar to their own. Those experiences provide greater credibility and impact than the experiences of someone who has no firsthand knowledge of living and working outside the United States. The personnel director who visits overseas operations during the best seasons—never during the monsoons or winter—and who always stays in the best hotels, eats at the best restaurants, is chauffeured around, and has his needs catered to by the local and expatriate staff is definitely not as effective as the personnel director who has been exposed to overseas living.

It was rewarding to find in our interviews that certain major multinationals in the fields of banking, oil, and consumer products have realized the value of field experience for their international personnel staffs. However, the majority of women we interviewed indicated that their spouses' companies had yet to realize this lesson and follow suit.

It was emphasized to us time and again that understanding attitudes and similar experiences on the parts of the company's international personnel director and staff increased contentment and understanding among expatriate employees and their families, which resulted in fewer failures, lengthier assignments for those already abroad, and tipped the scale favorably for those contemplating a first asssignment overseas.

As one of our respondents said:

The personnel manager for our division and area was required to move here. He had been in charge of international personnel matters for years, but it was his first experience of living abroad. He and his family went through the normal transfer traumas. His credibility went up one hundred percent in the eyes of all the company expatriates because, by the end of his two years with us, he knew what moving and living abroad were all about. His policy decisions from then on were influenced by personal understanding and were, therefore, more practical—for the company as well as for us.

Another interviewee remarked:

I have all the time in the world for the president of our company. He came up through the ranks and lived overseas for several years. He's lived in worse conditions than we have. When he makes policy decisions that affect the expatriate employees, their families know that he fully understands the ramifications.

And, as far as we are concerned, the best endorsement of a personnel director was:

The head of our international division, who was responsible for personnel decisions, lived abroad for a long time. He knows what it's really like. When visiting any of the overseas operations, he always makes time to meet informally and talk with the wives. We know that he knows how important we are; he makes us feel that our concerns and opinions are important to him and to the company.

Although such unqualified praise was not in the majority of comments made in our interviews, the praise clearly indicates that a multinational company has nothing to lose and much to gain in making sure that its international personnel staff has been properly exposed to the joys and rigors of living abroad.

Overseas Compensation

If compensation for the overseas employee could be characterized by one word, the word would be "controversial." There is no other aspect of being employed abroad that is more troublesome to the company, the employee, or the spouse than the compensation package. Parity, balance, objectivity, fairness, impartiality, equivalent standards, and equitable treatment are but some of the terms that are bandied about in the course of attempting to determine the salary and benefits which will be granted to the expatriate employee. This is a subjective issue for which no easy solutions exist. There are no magic formulas. Nor is it the aim of this chapter to elaborate on every possible benefit; but rather, we hope to entice you into investigating the employment policies and overseas compensation package of your company. The more you know about the compensation package, the better off you'll be. You'll know exactly where you stand with the company and you'll know exactly to what you are entitled.

Your company's overseas compensation policy manual will answer many of your questions and may provide solutions to many of the problems that might otherwise present a stumbling block to your family's adjustment. If the policy manual does not provide the answers you are looking for, you will at least have discovered your company's viewpoint on compensation. It may also be helpful to know as much as possible about comparable corporations and their compensation packages. Be careful, however. Policies vary from company to company. Try to avoid the trap of comparing your individual benefits to those of your friends; you must evaluate the total "net" package to compare "apples with apples."

Company policies are designed to cover a broad and general range of needs. Even if your company's policies are generous, you can expect that you and your family will have idiosyncratic problems and that you will have to go beyond the policies in order to solve them.

You should understand exactly what it is that you will receive from your company and why. If you don't, you may inadvertently step on toes by requesting more than is usually granted to that employee position, or you may end up not receiving all you are entitled to because you did not do your homework.

Finally, find out how flexible your company's policies are. There are always unforeseen events and situations for which you cannot plan in advance and you may have to return to the bargaining table after you've moved.

Designing Compensation Packages

Compensation is based on a variety of factors. What each employee will be entitled to may depend upon one or more of the following: company size and position in the industry; pay/benefit practices, both domestic and international; location of foreign operation; availability of qualified employees for the particular position; number of company employees already living abroad; taxes, domestic and host country; recruitment source; seniority; age; family size; employee grade level.

Many large, sophisticated companies assign grade levels to particular jobs; the grade levels, in turn, have salary ranges assigned to them. These salary ranges are updated periodically to maintain competitiveness with the rest of the marketplace. Therefore, when someone is hired for an overseas position, the company determines what the position's level is and therefore what the salary range is. The balance of the compensation package may include housing, cost of living adjustment (COLA), car, club memberships, private schools, home leaves, and tax equalization. Or the balance may be provided by an "overseas pay differential": one sum that is intended to cover all of the extras as opposed to specific individual categories.

Benefits

Through information derived from our survey, we have compiled the following list of the many possible benefits you may be entitled to as a result of an overseas transfer. Starred items are considered the most common.

Bonus*
Salaries (split compensation)*
Foreign service premiums
Hardship allowances
Profit sharing
Stock options
Pensions
Compensation for salary losses of wife
Assistance in finding employment overseas for the wife
Insurance*
Cost of living adjustment*
Currency adjustments*
Interest for loans and mortgages
Mortgage interest differentials
Tax equalization*
Relocation allowances*
Babysitting
Cancellation penalties
Realtor fees

Food
Furniture/appliance rental or purchase
Shipping, storage
House-hunting trip
Laundry
Legal fees
Documents and copying fees
Redecorating
Orientation programs
Translator
College education allowance for dependent children
Education allowance (grades 1–12)*
Automobiles
Charge Cards (travel and telephone)
Dues for professional and social societies
Expense account/entertainment
Housing/maintenance allowance*
Servants
Security personnel
Free products
Holidays (local and stateside)*
Home leaves*
Travel allowances
Severance package, including cost of return home

Cost of Living Adjustment (COLA)

A cost of living adjustment is generally paid by most corporations to equalize the difference, if any, for the cost of goods and services between the host country and the major cities of the United States. The main purpose of providing a COLA is to allow the expatriate the opportunity to live abroad at an equivalent standard to that which was maintained in the United States.

If you determine that your company will be providing a COLA, you may want to get answers to the following questions: How is the COLA calculated and paid? How often are company COLA surveys updated? Is the COLA taxable?

COLAs are not easy to determine. A number of factors are taken into consideration: the inflation rates of the host and home countries, the income level of the expatriate family, the size of the expatriate family, and the costs of comparable items at home and abroad.

Many companies use U.S. State Department studies to compute their COLAs. The State Department has four indexes: two are technical indexes, one is the effective index, and the other is the local index. The technical indexes should not be used for arriving at the COLA figure, nor should the effective index. The effective index applies to government employees who have the right to use commissaries and post exchanges and who have a variety of special privileges. The index which should be used is the *local index*. Check with your company to see which index it uses. Remember, State Department figures are based on the cost of living in Washington, D.C. If you come from a city with a lower cost of living than Washington, D.C., you may find yourself at a financial disadvantage. Of course, if you come from a city with a higher cost of living, you will find the statistics to be advantageous.

Education Allowance (Grades 1–12)

Free, quality public education does not exist in many parts of the world. The cost of education can be a heavy financial burden for parents if the costs are not to some extent covered by the corporation. A year of education for a child abroad can be as costly as a year at a fine stateside university. However, companies have long since learned that if they wish families to go and remain abroad, the companies will have to ensure that expatriate children receive a good education. Almost all multinational corporations contribute substantially or totally toward tuition and fees for local schooling. Most of these companies also pay for supplies. About half of the companies we know of pay full costs (tuition, room, and board) for boarding schools, and most of these also pay for one or two round trips home (wherever the family is) per year.

Ascertain exactly what the company policy is concerning your child's education. What costs will be covered in full or partially? Does the policy depend on the type of school? Will you or your child be entitled to reunion trips at company expense? If so, how many?

Home Leaves

Asked about home leaves and your company's policies concerning them. Almost everyone we surveyed felt that an annual home leave was an absolute necessity. One of the experienced expatriate wives we questioned said that new expatriates should not think that home leave is just an additional vacation, a time to relax. Quite the contrary. The three or four weeks that most companies give their expatriates as home leave are crammed with appointments—with doctors, dentists, lawyers, realtors, relatives, friends, and for much needed shopping—but no matter how hard you work during your home leave, you'll probably come nowhere near achieving everything you have to do. To top this off, many expatriates utilize part of their home leave to visit their headquarter's office, further reducing their leave time.

Ask any expatriate wife about home leaves and she'll heave a knowing sigh of exhaustion, laugh scornfully at anyone who would classify it under the heading of vacation, and vehemently declare, "Relaxation, my eye; it's strenuous and essential!"

Once again, if you don't want to end up in a financial bind, ask the following questions:

—What is the company's definition of home leave?
—Is the home leave your only vacation?

—What is the company's purpose for giving a home leave?

—How often is home leave given and to whom?

—What is the length of the home leave?

—What will be your mode and class of travel?

—Will the company pay for in-transit living expenses?

—What expenses during home leave will the company cover?

—Will the company provide you with a car?

—Or will you have access to a company car pool?

—Are national holidays considered part of home leave time?

—Where do you have to take your home leave?

—Can you be paid in lieu of taking home leave?

Home leave can be very costly. Few companies provide rental cars or per diem living allowances. Most families are on their own—hotels, car, food, laundry, all take their financial toll.

Where you take your home leave may even present a dilemma. Some companies require their expatriates to take their home leaves where the companies are head-quartered or where the expatriate lived prior to the over-seas assignment, even if there are no ties to the com-munity. Some companies also require that only part of the time be spent in the States and that the other part must be spent in the host country.

Housing Maintenance Allowance

While company benefits (or the lack thereof) frequently ignite some sort of controversy, the overseas housing al-lowance is without doubt the hottest issue. Find out all you can about housing costs in your prospective host country. As with every other element of a compensation package, the housing allowance should be understood in full by the employee and his spouse prior to departure. Ideally, it should be acceptable to everyone.

Questions you should ask are:

—What is the company's housing allowance policy?
—What specifically is the housing allowance supposed to cover (rent, security deposits, taxes, rental rights, maintenance utilities)?
—What are your company's definitions of "adequate housing" and "reasonable costs?"
—Is the housing allowance based on the average local housing costs or on the area which is most desirable for the expatriate?
—Is the housing allowance based upon rank, salary, size of family, availability of suitable housing?
—Is the allowance comparable to what other companies are paying?
—How is the allowance paid?
—If you are to reside in a company-leased or company-owned home, who will be responsible for the utilities and maintenance repairs?
—With what quality of furniture will you be expected to live?
—If you purchase a home overseas, will you receive loan assistance?
—Will you receive assistance to sell your host country home if the company asks you to relocate?
—If you purchase a host country home, will you still be entitled to housing allowance?
—If yes, how much housing allowance will you be entitled to?

Taxes and Tax Equalization

All United States citizens who work abroad are obligated by law to continue to pay personal income tax. Expatriates may also be required to pay personal income tax to the host country. However, although government policies seem to vary with each administration, expatriates are entitled to certain tax exemptions and foreign tax credits.

A tax credit permits the tax levied by a foreign government to be deducted from the U.S. tax liability—dollar for dollar. A word of caution is appropriate here. Tax structures fluctuate, and since many expatriates pay two personal income taxes, they often find themselves owing more money in taxes than they would in the United States. Many corporations have, therefore, devised tax equalization programs whereby expatriate employees do not pay taxes above and beyond those which they would pay in the States. When employees of such corporations reside in high-tax-rate countries, the corporations reimburse the employees for the excess payments, usually in monthly installments. When employees work in countries with low tax rates, their corporations often require them to remit their windfall tax "profits" via salary deductions.

There are a number of pamphlets available from the Internal Revenue Service, Washington, DC 20225, that can give you more information on the subject of taxes: "Tax Guide for Citizens Abroad," "Foreign Tax Credit for U.S. Citizens and Resident Aliens," "Tax Information Moving Expenses," and "Tax Guide for U.S. Citizens Employed in U.S. Possessions."

Or you can write to any of the major accounting firms to request their tax guides for expatriates. Frequently, multinational corporations offer tax services to their expatriates as a fringe benefit. Furthermore, many U.S. embassies have official tax representatives on their staffs—so you may have someone at hand to discuss taxes with while you are abroad.

Some fundamental questions that you should ask of

yourself, your company and your accountant or lawyer are:

- —Does the company have a tax equalization program?
- —If so, how is it administered?
- —What is considered taxable income by the IRS and by the tax authorities of the host country?
- —Will tax equalization have any negative effects on any bonus to which the employee may be entitled?
- —What about the effects on fringe benefits and allowances?
- —What tax exemptions and tax credits will you be entitled to as expatriates?
- —How will your taxes be paid?
- —How will your cash flow be handled in the event that you have to pay excess taxes throughout the year?
- —How will you be kept up to date on new tax laws which affect your situation?

Foreign Service Premiums and Hardship Allowances

Overseas premiums of one type or another are paid by about two thirds of the major multinationals to their expatriate employees. These premiums have two primary functions: they motivate employees to move abroad, and they encourage expatriate families to remain abroad.

More than half of the major multinationals also pay hardship allowances in certain locations. These allowances are based on a number of factors: inability to maintain a reasonable standard of living, risks to physical safety and health, difficult local language, minimal access to transportation, and climatic conditions.

Find out whether your company pays overseas premiums and/or hardship allowances. If so, make sure you understand how they are calculated and paid. Also find out whether these premiums are taxable and/or tax protected.

Insurance

There are several basic insurance questions that should be answered before you move:

—Will you and your family be completely insured—including hospitalization—while you are abroad?
—Will your stateside coverage continue while you are stationed overseas?
—To what extent will you be responsible for paying insurance premiums?
—To what extent will the corporation be responsible?
—How will the premium payments be made?
—How will the claim payments be made?
—Will your life insurance policies remain valid if you are to live in an area of civil unrest?
—If so, who will pay the additional high-risk premium, if there is one?
—If not, who will be responsible for purchasing new life insurance?

Orientation Programs

Multinational corporations have, with a few exceptions, been slow to realize the importance of orientation programs for the employees, let alone their families. Part of the problem is that most of the orientation programs are expensive—costing as much as U.S. $600 per day. However, these programs can produce well-informed expatriates who know what to expect and how to counteract culture shock and moving anxiety.

The best orientation programs include both pre-departure and on-site training. Pre-departure training should include language lessons and seminars on the host country's economic structure, political system, social customs, and business climate, as well as information on the living conditions the expatriates can expect. On-site training should include assistance with the details of establishing your new home. (Don't overlook the on-site training that you'll receive by tapping into the local grapevine.)

Orientation firms differ, not only in terms of what they charge and how long their courses are, but also in terms of what services they offer. You should also be aware of the fact that your corporation may not contract for all the services the orientation firms offer, feeling that only some of the services are really necessary.

Orientation services that most reputable firms offer may include the following: country orientation seminars; language lessons; descriptions of cities and neighborhoods; legal advice (pertaining to work permits, visas, leases, and customs); housing, decoration, and utilities installation assistance; assistance with pets; transportation system orientation; bilingual translators (for the settling-in period); school registration assistance; food shopping; and job search assistance for an employee's spouse.

If your company does provide an orientation program, try to take the time to critique it so that future expatriate employees will know what and what not to expect or so that the company will be able to find a better orientation program if necessary.

The Delicate Question of Negotiation

There are times when it is necessary to negotiate for what you need, for what is best for you and your family. *Before becoming an expatriate is one of those times.* Obviously, the employee should be the family's negotiator. But if you feel for some reason that you should become involved, by all means do so. Let's face it, you may understand the family's needs far better than anyone else and may therefore be better suited to the task. Or if your spouse—the employee—has already gone overseas, you may be the only person who can do the negotiating. Be diplomatic, and remember that you are not the employee; you are the stand-in. Even so, remember that the company needs you and your family because it needs your spouse. Don't be timid or intimidated. You have everything to gain and very little to lose. You have every right to discuss your concerns with the corporation and to solve the problems that face you in making the move.

You'll find the following tips and guidelines helpful, especially if you find yourself flying solo through the negotiations:

If you have not already met the personnel director, call and speak to him or her directly. The phone conversation may give you valuable insight into what sort of a person you'll be dealing with when you meet face to face.

Remember that the personnel director's time is valuable. Be prepared with written notes, and get to your points quickly.

Make sure that the subjects you discuss are needs and not wants. Your needs are of concern to the company; your wants should be of concern only to you.

Keep the conversation in plain English; don't let it slip into "corporatespeak," trade phrases, or terminology. Nor should you let your needs be discussed entirely in terms of corporate policy; you are there because you need special attention.

Do not become emotional; it will not help.

Dress appropriately for a business meeting, and maintain a positive frame of mind.

Above all, keep two things in mind: first, make sure your expectations are reasonable and in accord with your spouse's level in the corporate hierarchy; second, be prepared to give something as well. After all, that's what negotiation is all about—give and take.

Here is one example of a successful negotiation. A childless couple was asked to move to the Far East. Because her husband had to leave for the foreign assignment immediately, the wife was left to take care of everything, including the negotiation of benefits. Among other things, she succeeded in getting the company to pay for two annual home leaves. Everyone agreed that this was a good deal. The other candidate for the job had three children, and so moving him and his family would have cost the company a great deal more—with at least five round-trip airfares per year, plus education allowances and more costly housing.

Once again, if it's at all possible, the employee should do the negotiating. If you have to be involved, however, don't be daunted. The company needs you. You know what your family's needs are, and it's your responsibility to make sure that they are fulfilled.

CHAPTER XIX

The Role of the Expatriate Corporate Wife

"What do I do for the corporation? To begin with, I did move overseas. For me that meant temporarily putting my own career on hold. I realized it was foolish to complain about my circumstances. Instead, why not accept and enjoy them where I could?"

IF YOUR HUSBAND WORKS for a multinational corporation, an overseas assignment may involve more than simply relocating the family to a foreign location. Once you agree to accompany your spouse on an overseas assignment, knowingly or not, you have accepted certain obligations. To the uninitiated, most sound purely social. After your fifteenth trip to the pyramids with VIPs and their wives, however, you will realize that you are really a nonsalaried employee of your spouse's company. Unlike your spouse, however, you probably weren't provided with a job description prior to accepting the position.

Imagine a football coach briefing only the quarterback on the plays prior to the game. Obviously, the rest of the team would be unprepared to execute their responsibilities as the game developed. The analogy is appropriate for the expatriate family. When transferring an executive overseas, companies will almost always advise him on what lies ahead: the nature of his job, attendant problems, and what is expected of him. Numerous briefings, trips to the new territory, and exposure to the position are common in such transitions.

The physical move itself is only a small part of the expatriate *wife's* role. There are a multitude of other dimensions, few of which are clearly defined. It is important to realize that ambivalence, conflicting demands and inconsistencies will continue to surface as you establish your home abroad; and, lacking clarification, it will be up to you to determine just what your role will encompass. One source of good advice is other experienced and successful expatriate wives. Talk to them, including wives from other corporations. For this advice to be relevant, make sure that their relative standing (based on their husbands' positions within their corporations) is equal to your own or has been in the recent past. Another excellent source is your husband. Talk to him about the company—what he believes is expected of you and how he feels about it. Last, talk to the company itself; your husband's boss or his wife may be able to put your mind at ease on many matters. Treat the process as though you were researching a prospective job.

Of course, you do not have to accept the advice of others. Many women have their own careers or outside personal interests. There are also those whose children and homes will always be their first and only consideration. Frequently, there is nothing wrong with choosing to avoid corporate responsibilities and that decision should not be an impediment to your husband's career. In fact, the corporation itself may prefer wives to remain distant from the business world or to appear only at quasi-social occasions. Our survey, however, indicates that this tends to be the exception rather than the rule.

Keep in mind that it will be necessary to reestablish your role with each move and promotion. Your husband's progression along the corporate ladder may require adjustments for the entire family. There will be times when you will be called upon to take on a more active role in company affairs. Your husband's new position may necessitate your traveling with him more frequently. Your social duties may necessitate more formal corporate entertainment. Or, given your spouse's additional responsibilities, you may simply have to assume a more solitary and dominant role in the management of the family.

Key Accountabilities

Assuming you have not had the opportunity to research your role as an expatriate corporate wife or have done so and drawn a blank, what are some of the accountabilities likely to be expected of you?

Acting as Hostess

Our survey results indicate that the majority of expatriate corporate wives are expected to host the occasional dinner party or reception for visiting dignitaries. Most wives are also expected to attend dinners and receptions—suitably charming, well coiffed, and attractively attired.

The wife's presence at such affairs serves several purposes: to develop and cement employee/corporation relationships, to further business/client contacts in a casual and friendly atmosphere, to limit the discussion of purely business subjects, and to provide an opportunity for subordinates and superiors to communicate in a casual, relaxed environment.

These responsibilities may not be different from those of the stateside corporate wife. It is the process of fulfilling the responsibilities that may differ quite dramatically. One woman related a story of generosity that went totally unknown and unappreciated by her guests:

> While we were stationed in Africa, I was asked to host a dinner for a large group of VIPs visiting from the U.S. By the time the guest list was completed I had more than forty people to feed. Our area of the country had a scarcity of meat and poultry, and, living far from the sea, fish was nonexistent. We had learned to cope with this by buying and freezing these goods whenever they were available.
>
> By using every bit of meat and poultry in my freezer and by asking some of the other company wives to contribute to the dinner, we were able to stretch our stores, offering a mixed buffet menu.
>
> Our guests, many of whom had never lived outside the United States, enjoyed their meal, never realizing the amount of effort it took to feed them. Nor did they ever know that their African hosts would be eating beans and vegetables for a month, until the next shipment of meat was due to arrive.

Attending Conventions

An extension of the expatriate wife's role as a hostess is often the expectation that she will represent the company at meetings and conventions. It was not uncommon in our survey to hear of wives who were called upon to attend as many as six conventions a year. While this may sound like a perpetual vacation to some, attending conventions, which typically last for three or four days, requires a significant commitment of time, energy, and effort. It is *work*. Being wined and dined until 4 a.m., then rising bright eyed to catch the 8 a.m. bus tour with clients' wives, and later circulating among your husband's associates and guests demands stamina, devotion, and concentration.

Lest one think the solution is as simple as politely declining the next invitation, we relate another wife's story:

> We were living in a country with beautiful seaside resorts; but after the fourth convention in a row at the same place, believe me, I was having difficulty drumming up any enthusiasm about going. I even asked my husband if I could plead illness and stay at home. He looked at me in total disbelief and reminded me that most women would gladly give anything for the chance to go—not to mention the fact that my absence would be all too noticeable to the company.

For the expatriate wife attending her first *international* convention, it is advisable to pay attention to a number of details. Ask for and examine the agenda. Inquire into the clothing and social customs of the host city well in advance so that you will be properly attired and prepared for all the events.

Your job is to particpate in the scheduled events for the wives. Although you may dislike visiting museums, the acquaintances you will make during these events could become good friends in a foreign land (or possibly good business contacts for your husband).

Finally, self-sufficiency at conventions is a must. It may not be possible to get your hair and nails done for the big night. Bring your dual voltage travel iron, hair dryer, a good book, and your needlepoint. These are the types of tools that you may need. Remember, your husband may have little time to spend with you. You are both there on business. Be prepared to be independent.

Meetings and conventions can be a great opportunity for personal growth as well. Each new convention location will add to your knowledge of other cultures and languages. If you should find yourself at a convention where there is a lack of planned activities for the wives, you may want to take matters into your own hands. Gather a group for sight seeing, or organize card games, tennis matches, or exercise groups. Don't hesitate to initiate a group discussion on a topic of mutual interest, such as an outline of suggested activities for the next convention.

Community Involvement

Less frequent accountabilities for the expatriate wife are expectations that wives be active participants in non-controversial community affairs. Signing on as den mothers for the scouts, serving on the PTA, or collecting funds for charity are but a few available activities. Some companies have even been known to include the wife's community activities as part of her husband's performance review and assessment of cultural adaptability.

The following story illustrates what can develop from a simple community activity, benefiting everyone along the way:

The women's club I belonged to overseas had, as its major charity event, a spring craft bazaar. Hosted by the club, charitable organizations from all over the country were invited to set up booths and sell their handicrafts. It became apparent that many of these groups could profit from being able to supply handicrafts year round but that they needed an outlet. With a small committee of talented and dedicated ladies, our craft center was started.

The center developed rapidly, as many members of the club gave of their talents to help local organizations refine their products. Other volunteers located, decorated, and staffed the shop. The center was an overnight success. Many cottage industries gained financially, and many volunteers achieved personal satisfaction. The P.R. benefits and goodwill our companies derived from our work were uncountable.

Twenty-four-Hour Staff Assistant

Probably the least recognized, yet most critical, accountability for the expatriate wife is that of being a round-the-clock staff assistant to her husband. He, too, is living and working in a foreign environment and, despite preparation by the company, still has needs that are not usually encountered in a domestic assignment. One of these needs may be his tendency to bring office work home with him, seeking your assistance. This may be due to the lack of skilled clerical personnel or to genuine concerns of confidentiality. Many of the women surveyed said they often spent hours typing and proofreading their husbands' reports. In some cases they could help with the translation of international correspondence. In others, they simply knew how to spell in English. Presentations seem to be an integral part of overseas transactions, and many wives find themselves acting as their husbands' speech coaches. Listening to the same speech over and over again may be tedious, but one fact remains: there may be no one else to whom he can turn.

You may also find yourself acting as your husband's sounding board, because the expatriate man often has few, if any, people at the office with whom he can share his private thoughts. This is especially true when the foreign office is staffed with local employees and the expatriate is the only representative of the home office. Local hires and third-country nationals generally have difficulty aligning themselves professionally and personally with the expatriate, as he is most often their boss and of a different culture. Thus it falls to the wife to listen to her husband and to help him sort through his thoughts. The wife must extend this listening service far beyond the normal focus on people problems. This does not mean that you will or should make the decisions that are your husband's responsibility; but you can have a significant input. With good sense and intuition you may very well develop valuable relations where none existed before and establish new bonds with your spouse.

Training New Arrivals

Your husband and the corporation may expect you to offer assistance to new expatriate wives in your company who arrive in your area. Knowing what you have been through because of your own move, you may be more than willing to do this. Such assistance does promote a sense of comraderie among company wives. Be aware, though, the continuous contact can be somewhat stifling. According to our survey, the old adage "familiarity breeds contempt" often holds true in small foreign communities. For a number of reasons, most wives find it preferable to keep a certain amount of social distance between themselves and other wives in the corporation. This is just as true for the stateside wife as for the expatriate wife. While your hand should be outstretched in the event of a special occasion or emergency, for the most part your intimate friends may well be found outside of your own corporate family.

Social Secretary

Invariably, once the family has settled into its new country, the expatriate wife finds that she is responsible for establishing not only her own social network but also the networks of her children and her husband. It seems to be a fact of life abroad that most people work more hours per day than they did in the States. Expatriate employees, therefore, have very little time to develop the friendships that they would like. Beyond initiating and establishing social contacts for the family, you may also be in a position to meet and cultivate influential people who can assist your husband in business. The international community is generally quite small, and networking is a valuable tool.

Success Profile of the Expatriate Wife

With the job description in mind, it is appropriate to describe the attributes one would expect to find in the successful expatriate wife. There are no right or wrong answers, nor is there a scientific method of determining the ideal profile. Nonetheless, the consensus of our survey indicated there are particular characteristics and traits associated with success among wives living abroad.

The most fundamental quality for successful living abroad is also the most obvious: namely, the willingness to uproot one's family and establish a new life style overseas. Closely akin to this are the characteristics of flexibility, adaptability, and the capacity to compromise. Patience is a virtue no matter where you live; but the opportunities for testing it are vastly greater overseas. A good sense of humor is a particularly useful asset; independence, initiative, and high stress tolerance are other pluses. A facility and desire for new experiences is the icing on the cake.

Fear not if you don't have all of these qualities. Many are developed and refined as you experience overseas living, and practice makes perfect.

CHAPTER XX

Corporate Accountabilities: How Your Company Can Help

A N EXECUTIVE'S CREDENTIALS, STATUS, AND AUTHORITY
are readily transferable. They go with him as automatically as his personnel records, aiding and supporting
him as he becomes ensconced in his new surroundings.
Day-to-day work, more than likely, is conducted in English. His support staff at the new office will usually en-
deavor to do everything possible to ease his transition,
often sheltering him from the realities of life outside the
office.

By comparison, relatively few of the expatriate wives
surveyed considered themselves adequately prepared to
execute *their* responsibilities in the transition. For example, over half of the women we interviewed said they were

responsible for the family's physical moves. In many cases, wives were left to their own devices in managing the myriad details of the move and the stress resulting from the uncertainty of the transfer. Most wives believed they could have served their husbands' interests (and their husbands' companies) better had they received greater guidance as to what needed to be done and where to find the resources to do it.

It is generally accepted that over eighty percent of re-locations that fail are attributable to family, rather than professional, pressures and problems. Adequate guidance and support would significantly reduce the risk of such failures and have a positive financial impact. The cost of transferring a family abroad runs between $50,000 and $150,000 (for expenses including house-hunting trips, furniture shipments, interim hotel and living arrange-ments, and employee transfer allowances). This expendi-ture does not include the less visible costs of recruiting, selecting, and training key managers. With the stakes of failure so high, it would seem prudent for corporations to increase their efforts to better prepare the women who are responsible for creating a stable, supportive family en-vironment.

Training Sessions Before the Transition

According to the results of our survey, corporations should provide training sessions for their employees' wives. These sessions should cover specific elements of the assignment and provide comprehensive information about the foreign location. Sessions should also cover the corporation's background, functions, and structure.

A partial list of topics that should be discussed in-cludes: what the corporation expects of its employees and their families (specifically, the wives); why U.S. employees are being sent abroad; company policies and procedures (both domestic and international); normal hours and work week in the host country; local customs and social values; climate and clothing suggestions.

Also, political conditions; currency and customs regulations; documentation requirements; health regulations and precautions; transportation systems; facilities, products, and services (what's available and what's not, such as electricity, potable water, telephones, paved roads, pollution control systems); typical natural disasters (and contingency plans for unexpected events).

International Personnel Staffing

Successful expatriation depends as much upon knowledgeable home-office support as it does upon the individuals in the field. The most important attribute of an international personnel staff (from the wives' perspective) is a genuine concern for the expatriate employee's family. If that concern is not evident, the family will feel isolated and less motivated to make the overseas assignment a success.

The professionalism of competent international personnel staffs is seen in their willingness to listen and respond effectively to the questions and requests of expatriate wives and their families. These staffs ensure that expatriates receive on-site, as well as pre-departure, support. They are also aware of the availability and reliability of relocation services where employees will be residing. Files are maintained and frequently updated as to the social, political, and economic environments. Finally, there is always at least one person on the staff who has had firsthand knowledge of the overseas living experience. If your spouse's company fits this profile, you are off to a very good start.

PART SIX

CHAPTER XXI

Repatriation—An Overview

REPATRIATION IS THE ALL-ENCOMPASSING TERM used to define the multitude of physical and psychological factors associated with the expatriate family's return home at the end of its overseas assignment. While repatriation is a straightforward concept, it is laden with strong and varied emotions. It connotes joy, fulfillment, and a sense of completion. Repatriation also causes feelings of anxiety, sadness, loss, or apprehension.

Most expatriates realize that their foreign assignment will come to an end at some point in time, and that they will return to the United States. Some even know their specific repatriation date and destination prior to moving abroad. The vast majority, however, are unaware of when the call will come, and have given the subject of repatriation little thought. Consequently, the call to repatriate typically comes as a surprise, and begins yet another period of transition and adjustment. For the spouse-employee, repatriation means a change in position, job responsibilities, and perhaps company affiliation. For the wife, repatriation is an uprooting of the home, social environment, and support systems she has worked so hard to establish for the family. For the children, repatriation means new schools, new friends, and new experiences. Nonetheless, while any move is onerous, "going home" is usually viewed with excitement and anticipation.

Why Do People Repatriate?

The reasons for repatriation are as numerous and varied as the reasons for having moved abroad in the first place. Again, they tend to fall into two general categories: corporate and personal. As with the decision to go abroad, the prime instigating factor is usually a managerial decision: the employee's services are desired back in the States. Of course, in some cases, the decision to repatriate is initiated by the expatriate for personal reasons.

According to our survey, the majority of company-instigated repatriations are a result of:

—Filling a vacancy in the home office;
—Change of the company's international policy or organizational structure;
—Personal and professional advancement of the employee;
—Non-renewal of the employee's work or residence permit by the host country;
—Replacement of the employee by a local national; and
—Inability to perform up to corporate expectations.

For the families that repatriate for personal reasons, the most common—yet most difficult to articulate—reason is the feeling of a need to "return home" or to be an "American in America again." For some expatriates, this feeling occurs when the children have left the nest abroad to attend college. For others, there is simply a time when the family senses a need to get back to familiar surroundings. As two seasoned expatriate wives in our survey put it:

> There wasn't any real reason why we wanted to go home, but the idea and desire just kept growing inside of us. We'd been abroad for eight years, lived in three different countries, mastered two foreign languages, and three unique cultures. We could have continued living abroad, but we just felt we wanted to get back—to be "home."

*   *   *

> After fifteen years abroad in various assignments, we just wanted to be Americans again (whatever that means). Maybe we were tired of the feeling of being foreigners, I don't really know. But we knew it was time for us to go home.

For many families in our survey, this vague, nebulous feeling—alone or coupled with other personal motivations—served as the only rationale for their repatriation.

Of the more specific personal reasons mentioned for repatriating, the strongest and most compelling revolved around the children of the family. Several families we interviewed returned to the United States in order to enhance the lives of their children or facilitate their development. Some wanted their children to have the opportunity "to know America," to experience American education, sports, cultural and social values before becoming adults. Having lived abroad already, the parents reasoned, repatriation would afford them "the best of both worlds." Other families found it necessary to address the special needs of a child, such as physical, mental, social, or educational deficiencies. In more than a few cases, the need existed to establish the children's American citizenship, since they had been born and lived overseas all of their lives.

Concern for the well-being of children tends to occur most frequently in the teenage years. This is the point in time when most expatriate parents examine the pros and cons of living abroad, and evaluate the advantages and disadvantages of foreign living for their children. Critical factors to be considered are the potential disruption of the children's social and educational development if another move should occur. Continuity of academic and extracurricular credentials, and emotional and psychological adaptation are critical concerns. It is at this stage that some parents opt to return to the States in order to provide their children with a period of stability prior to entering their college years or entering the work force. Other families have the more practical motivation of establishing state residency in order to take advantage of subsidized education, technical or vocational training.

Other personal reasons for repatriation were attributed to some combination of:

—Boredom
—Anxiety
—Marital difficulties
—Inability to come to terms with culture shock
—Health problems
—Aging parents
—Civil unrest and concerns over personal safety
—Accomplishment (or shortfall) of financial goals

A few returned simply because they could not find what they were searching for when they decided to go abroad.

Reverse Culture Shock

Yes, you will experience culture shock again. Remember that strange feeling of moving to a foreign land and being confronted by a different language, a different set of values and standards, a different way of thinking and living? Well, all those differences will face you again with your repatriation. Remember the months of coping, adapting, and adjusting your lifestyle to accommodate your new environs? Well, get ready to repeat the process. Can it be? Believe it. To expatriates, reverse culture shock is probably the most surprising aspect of returning home. As one of our interviewees explained:

> When you move to a foreign country, you expect things to be different. You are ready to be flexible and accept whatever comes along. When you go home, however, you expect things to be much as they were when you left. They're not. A simple matter, like getting my state driver's licence became a major production. I failed my first two attempts: once for a quick change of lanes during my driving test, and once for leaning on my horn—both typical Caracas driving techniques.

Truly, life never stands still. Your hometown or city will certainly have changed while you were away. Your friends will have changed. And, most importantly, you will have changed—in many more ways than you would ever imagine. Experiences, concerns, and opinions you once shared with friends and neighbors may no longer provide a common bond. New activities, priorities, and values will have entered your life and are relevant to you—but not necessarily to your old acquaintances. Your time abroad will have made you a different person, modifying your interests and behavior. By the same token, your friends and associates will have gone through similar transformations, increasing the disparity of dated memories.

Admittedly, it is quite difficult to recognize and comprehend the changes that have taken place within yourself and your family. You have been too close, too involved, and have not had a vantage point from which to observe the modifications. The reverse is true, however, of your vision of "home." You will immediately notice that "home" is not what it was when you left. But don't despair. It is simply part of culture shock in reverse and by now you're an old pro at handling it. As one repatriated gal told us:

> I was elated when I learned we were returning to the same hometown and the very same house, which we had rented out. We were coming "home" and things could not have seemed simpler. I was rudely shaken out of my complacency, however, on my first trip to my favorite supermarket. As I pulled out of the same old parking lot onto the same old street, I was horrified to see two lanes of traffic bearing down on me. As the policeman explained, the street had been made one-way in my absence.

*   *   *

Another newly repatriated wife related this tale:

> When I returned to the States, I was truly frustrated by the lack of interest my new neighbors had concerning events of global significance. Granted, I was coming back from a "heady" life of socializing with foreign dignitaries and ambassadors. But even our expatriate women's club coffee hour topics in-

cluded the unrest in the Middle East and in Central America, the opening up of Germany, and the drug problems on the U.S. border. When I mentioned these subjects at luncheons or dinner parties, people listened for a moment, smiled politely and quickly changed the subject to which streets in town needed repaving or who was the latest divorcée. I was dumbfounded by their priorities.

*   *   *

Another woman told us of her frustrations in the supermarket. There were just so many choices to make vis-a-vis brands and sizes, plus a myriad of new products, that shopping was a major project.

As these stories illustrate, repatriation portends another period of reorientation and readjustment. Our interviews and personal experience confirm that few escape the reverse culture shock associated with repatriation. Most find the transition can be facilitated by following a few simple procedures. First, think of your stateside move as yet another relocation to another foreign country. Realize that, in many ways, the United States will be foreign to you, especially if you have been abroad for several years. Approach the different stages of relocation with the wisdom and insight gleaned from your previous international move(s). Capitalize on your experience; yet, remember, no two transfers are the same, despite superficial similarities; nor does repatriation neatly conform to any familiar pattern. Be just as sensitive to what is taking place during your repatriation as you were during expatriation. Maintain your flexibility, perspective and, most importantly, your sense of humor.

CHAPTER XXII

Family Adjustments

IN REPATRIATION, AS WITH YOUR MOVE ABROAD, your first concern after finding a home, schools for your children, and coping with the physical move, will probably be your family's readjustment.

The Children

Your children may experience many of the same problems that they faced when they made their overseas move(s). They may encounter a different style of education. They may need to repeat a year of school, or they may be so far ahead of their age group that they may skip a year, or they may go on to advanced studies in some subjects. They may have to learn new sports, new styles of dance, new slang, new mannerisms, and maybe even change their style of dress and hair. Bear with them and help them draw out the best from their international experience.

Regardless of age, their experiences abroad will have made them unique, and broadened their perspectives.

Help your children promote what they have gained from living abroad. Foster their individual talents, interests, abilities, and skills. Encourage them to share their experiences with their peers and others, and to use their newly developed maturity and sophistication to best advantage.

One former expatriate told us of an experience with her son upon moving back to the United States after living in Brazil for a number of years:

> Our son was anxious to play sports, but he was intimidated by his friends and their abilities on the football field. They'd all been playing the game for years and it was too late for a "beginner" to join. He'd had years of playing soccer, and was quite good, but the game had not yet become popular here. One evening we discussed ideas of how to promote soccer, since there certainly seemed to be enough kids who might enjoy it. I checked with the town parks commission and was told we could use the town's community field for games if other parents and kids were interested. From there we all dug in. My husband recruited other fathers to help coach, our son spread the word around school of a new "soccer program" and I handled the P.R. and community support. Over the years, the soccer program has grown tremendously and now there are hundreds of kids of all ages playing in a number of different leagues.

As with most children, yours may feel somewhat uncomfortable for a while. Assure them that this is normal, and do whatever you can to help them find their new niche in the world. Make a point of introducing yourself to their teachers, counselors, and anyone who may have an impact on their school day. Make sure their school(s) are aware of where you have been and how you expect your children's experience and new skills to be chan-

nelled in the short and long term. Our research shows that
with encouragement and support, children will achieve
success in their own ways. A child's sense of self worth is
extremely fragile, and you can and should do everything
possible to monitor and nurture it during repatriation, regardless of how comfortable you feel in your new surroundings.

Your Husband

While your first efforts may be directed at helping your
children through their adjustments, do not forget to be
sensitive to your husband's needs. The process of repatriation can be more difficult for him than moving abroad had
been. Besides dealing with the changes in your home
community, and among your friends, as well as the financial ramifications of the move, he may also find little
glamour in returning to the home office.

More often than not, changes have taken place in his
"old" corporate environment. There may be many new
faces, and changes in the organizational structure to absorb. The support systems he had developed before going
abroad may need to be rebuilt. The importance of the
company's international business may be only a small
part of the business as a whole. Remember, it is difficult
for anyone to go from being a "key player" of the company
abroad to being "one of many" employees at home, even if
repatriation was the result of a promotion. Again, you may
be his best sounding board as he sorts out the meta-
morphosis that has taken place.

Think of Yourself

Sooner or later in the repatriation process your thoughts will turn to yourself. It is at this point you may ask, "Where have I been? What have I become? And where am I going with my own life?"

Where have you been? Regardless of the geographical area, you have very probably had the greatest and most personally broadening experience of your life.

What have you become? This will certainly depend on what you gained from, and how you dealt with your experiences while living abroad. More than likely, you have become more educated and worldly, maybe even more sophisticated, understanding, and sensitive. You certainly have learned more about yourself and your own strengths and weaknesses. In some cases you may have developed emotional strengths and physical skills you had never considered possible. But there is no doubt you have grown and changed, and you surely should be a better person in many ways, and all due to the experience of having dealt with moving and living abroad.

Where are you going? If you worked before you moved abroad, you may want to resume your career. If you worked while living overseas, you may want to continue your career now that you are home. Keep in mind that, in either case, you may encounter many of the readjustment problems your spouse is confronting in the workplace. Whether returning to work, continuing to work, or beginning a new career, the experiences and skills you have gained while living abroad will certainly enhance your resumé. You may very well find new career opportunities open to you, and it is an ideal time to consider them all.

Look at us for example, your authors: we were not professional writers. But we had learned so much about moving and living abroad, and so much of it was common to any international move that we were determined to share our knowledge and experiences. We hoped to make the expatriate adventure a little easier and a lot more understandable, and to create a great deal of happy memories.

For the many women returning home who will not "work" there are still options and opportunities to be explored and developed. Most of the women we interviewed were determined in some way to share their international experiences with others. Some of the most popular suggestions were:

—Teach English to foreigners;
—Keep up their new language skills;
—Teach the foreign language;
—Give talks or slide/video presentations on the former host country;
—Teach the cooking of foreign food;
—Teach foreign handicrafts;
—Work on promoting international exchange of students and culture;
—Give guided tours to the former host country;
—Import and sell foreign handicrafts, art or antiques.

For the majority of the women we interviewed, "coming home" felt like retiring from active duty. Many of them said that they missed the involvement with their spouses' companies. However, these women also anticipated very little trouble in building an identity of their own. Almost all of those polled said they missed the excitement of living overseas and, for most, the benefits derived from the experience far outweighed any low points that they might have experienced. As was prescribed for your husband and children, take what you have gained from living overseas, add it to what you were, and go from there. The future is wide open and now is a great opportunity to capitalize on it.

CHAPTER XXIII

Financial Ramifications of Repatriation

IN ADDITION TO REALIZING THAT reverse culture shock can be a major adjustment associated with your repatriation, you may also discover that the financial impact of your return can be equally dramatic. For most, it is "reverse financial shock." Many of the perks, benefits and monetary inducements that influence your decision to go abroad now come to an abrupt halt. Housing and educational allowances, cost of living differentials, home leaves, company cars, and household help are a thing of the past. In theory, all of these "extras" were required to bring you to economic and social parity with life in the United States. In fact, most expatriates come to institutionalize these benefits while they are abroad and are disappointed to lose them when they return home. Our advice is to accept the loss of these "extras" as a trade-off. It's a question of compromise, of pluses and minuses, which should be viewed philosophically. While you no longer receive financial assistance for your children's private education, you are now in a position to select a school system that offers free public education. In its totality, whether you win or lose is really a function of your peace of mind and sense of fulfillment; not the dollars and cents.

According to our survey, the financial implications of returning home impact most in three areas. First, and most readily apparent, is the termination of monetary perquisites. Second, is the need to re-establish the material aspects of your life, such as housing, appliances, cars, and the like. Third, and most subtle, is the modification required in your style of living.

Life Without Allowances

Depending upon your employer's particular compensation program, you were offered certain financial inducements while you lived abroad. These may have included housing assistance, a cost of living differential, tax equalization, schooling support, an overseas premium, a moving allowance and/or numerous other variations on the theme. The primary objectives of these payments were:

—To reimburse you for expenses that you would not have incurred had you remained in the States;
—To enable you to maintain a standard of living comparable to that you were leaving behind;
—To compensate you for accepting the trials and tribulations associated with living outside of the United States;
—To induce you to move in the first place.

The majority of expatriates find living abroad to be financially attractive. In fact, through various techniques—such as renting their stateside homes and watching their pennies—expatriates find that they are able to save significantly more money abroad than they could in the States. As one expatriate summed it up:

> It was great while it lasted! In our five years abroad, we lived well and still built a larger nest egg than would have been possible working in the United States.

As you contemplate your return home in financial terms, a word of caution is in order. Most of us get used to our levels of income, and develop spending and saving patterns accordingly. To the extent you have built your overseas allowances into your economic lifestyle (or taken them for granted), their termination will be proportionately more traumatic. Therefore, before repatriating and locking in major financial commitments, analyze your pending remuneration package and develop a budget that accommodates the loss of your international benefits. Since "net" income is what is available to spend, make sure you run your numbers on an after-tax basis. With tax laws changing as rapidly as they are, it would be advisable to get professional assistance.

When developing your stateside budget, a host of expense categories need to be estimated and forecast. In addition to the standard rent or mortgage, food, transportation, telephone, clothing, medical, dental, gifts, and contributions, don't forget to include:

—Homeowner and auto insurance, not carried abroad;
—Heat, light and electricity, which may have been; included in the rent;
—Vacations and travel, previously covered by home leave allowances;

—Social club membership fees and dues;
—Charitable contributions;
—State sales and income taxes, not incurred overseas; and,
—Sundry other items such as water, refuse collection, lawn maintenance, snow removal, childcare, and the like.

It is wise to anticipate what your expenses will be back in the States and to budget accordingly. Many new categories of expense items are going to take a bite out of your disposable income, and you will want to plan carefully.

Reestablishing Your Asset Base

According to our respondents, the next most important financial aspect of repatriation is the need to reestablish your asset base in the States. Clearly, housing is the biggest dollar item to be considered. The majority of expatriate families have leased their housing abroad, but want to own their home when they return. For some, their old homestead awaits. Others may want to sell their previous homes and move into different quarters. Still others sold their homes when they went abroad and now have to tap their savings and investments to become home owners again. Neither housing prices nor mortgage rates are likely to be what they were when you left and such changes can be shocking.

Transportation is another large item. Some expatriates owned cars abroad, but are unlikely to have shipped them home. Some had company cars, which is not a perk of their stateside position. Others simply did without while living abroad. Now, a car for Dad, another for Mom, and possibly one for the older children can cost what a two bedroom home did when you went overseas.

Household furniture and appliances is a third category of major expense when returning to the States. A new table and chairs may be appropriate for the size of the new dining room; a new sofa may be required to replace the old one that would not have survived the move; or, new beds with mattresses that don't sag to the floor may be necessary. Frequently, appliances have to be replaced, since the 220 voltage required in many overseas countries won't operate in the States. Refrigerators, stoves, washers, dryers, computers, clocks, blenders, microwaves, TVs, VCRs, and CD players all fit this description. When you add it up, you may discover the meaning of "sticker shock."

An "all other" category of items that may need to be acquired or replaced might include curtains and drapes, carpeting, and telephones; and lamps may need to be re-wired. Not to be overlooked is clothing. Moving from Brazil to Minneapolis may mean a "total rehab" of the wardrobe; not just Mom's and Dad's, but the kids' as well. Even if the climate is similar, the styles and sizes are probably not.

Your New Lifestyle

One of the more subtle aspects of repatriation is the tug-of-war it creates in your lifestyle. Respondents in our survey found it hard to articulate and difficult to quantify, but most experienced the same phenomenon. Depending upon your length of time overseas, you will have come to expect a certain standard of living. Upon your return to the States, financial and cultural changes are likely to dictate a behavioral change. Much like "life without allowances," only in a qualitative sense, many of the support systems for your international lifestyle are withdrawn. The question then becomes, "Do you want to, can you afford to, maintain the style of living you have come to enjoy abroad?"

In many respects, the expatriate lifestyle is higher, faster, and fuller than that experienced in the States. This tends to be a function of several dynamics. First, most expatriate families receive numerous financial benefits, as discussed earlier in this book. Second, many expatriates tend to have significantly greater disposable income than their local national associates. Third, expatriate families tend to seek out new adventures and novel experiences, taking full advantage of their new environs. And, fourth, many countries have pleasant "lifestyle perks" inherent in their cultures. The common use of servants outside of the United States is an obvious example. Many of these benefits serve as compensation for living in a foreign land and grappling with a strange culture. The flip side of the coin is that these benefits do, in fact, raise the expatriate's standard of living and provide an elevated lifestyle not experienced back home.

The availability and affordability of servants is the most frequently cited example of international lifestyle "perks." An upstairs maid, downstairs maid, butler, cook, driver, and gardener may be a bit of an exaggeration (though not necessarily so in India); but having at least one servant is a benefit many expatriate families enjoy. (Just the thought of going straight to bed after a dinner party, then waking up to find the dishes done and house spotless, makes these authors sigh.) Company cars, corporate club memberships, and entertainment at company expense are other lifestyle features soon taken for granted while living abroad. Company-paid travel, conventions in exotic locations, sightseeing, and hobnobbing with dignitaries and the "jet set" round out the list of typically mentioned benefits. As one executive groaned:

You should have seen me last weekend. Instead of

18 holes of golf, I spent all Saturday and most of Sunday working in the yard. And to think I fired my gardener in Mexico because he wanted a small raise! The way my muscles felt on Monday morning, I would have sent him a first class ticket to come here.

CHAPTER XXIV

Choices

NOW THAT YOU'VE HAD A GLIMPSE of what to expect, and
understand the concept of repatriation a little better,
there is one more thought to keep in mind. You still have
major choices and decisions to make. The first and most
significant is, "Do you really want to return to the United
States?" There are alternatives open to you and the answer
need not be an automatic "yes." Or, assuming you do wish
to return, the entire spectrum of options associated with
any move is available to you again.

To Stay or to Go

If you are enjoying the experience of living abroad and
really do not want to return to the States right away, the
spouse-employee may be able to negotiate other options
with his employer. These include:

—Declining the transfer;
—Asking for a lateral transfer and relocation to another
overseas posting;

—Requesting a postponement of the repatriation date; or,

—Determining if the current job and location can be combined with or expanded to encompass the new responsibilities.

For a few, the desire to remain abroad may be so strong that the spouse-employee would rather change companies than repatriate. This is obviously a dramatic decision; but it may be an option available to you. In other cases, the circumstances might merit the spouse-employee repatriating on his own, leaving the family abroad. This proved to be the optimal solution for one family we interviewed. As the wife related:

> After two years of living here, my husband was recalled to the States to be trained in the latest technology for our company's products. We knew this would take about a year and then he would be reposted here. It seemed best if the children and I stayed on, rather than disrupt their schooling and social lives. I'm glad we did it. The time flew by and now we're together again.

Other families have resigned themselves to repatriation, only to find that international blood continued to course through their veins. The lure of living abroad is apparent in the following woman's story:

> I couldn't believe my husband really wanted to leave! We had spent almost all of our married life in Latin America. One day he announced that we were "going home" to a place where the children would have to go to public schools. We couldn't afford our maid or driver, and I would have to cook! Well, we

tried it for a year and then he requested a transfer back to South America. I've often wondered if it was my cooking?

Another gal told us:

> I couldn't wait to move back to our house in the States. All I could think about while we lived in Paris was how nice it would be to go home. Once we were back, I realized what we had given up in terms of travel, excitement, and daily adventures. There was so much to do that I simply took for granted. We put in for reassignment abroad and are so much happier to be overseas again.

As we stated in an earlier chapter, repatriation is sometimes initiated by the expatriate family for personal reasons. This is frequently motivated by a concern for the children—their health, well-being, or education. Yet repatriation need not be the only answer. An analysis of why a particular family member would be better off in the States and what is lacking in your host country may suggest other alternatives to relocating the entire family. This type of problem is most frequently confronted by families who live in areas of the world where educational systems are deficient. It may be that schooling is only available through the eighth grade, or the quality of teaching is substandard. Expatriate families who do not wish to return to the United States (or cannot for employment reasons) will find that boarding schools and colleges are obvious options. These do not necessarily have to be in the States. There may be schools, colleges or vocational training institutions in neighboring countries that are more than adequate and much closer to the expatriate family's host country. Another alternative would be to send the child to live in the States with family or friends. College-aged children are usually happy to live on their own or in college housing. One family told us:

> The American school in our host country only went through eighth grade. When Tommy was ready for ninth, we thought it meant all five of us moving home, sacrificing a wonderful career opportunity and exciting life for the rest of the family. Our company personnel director suggested that we consider boarding school for our son in England. The company would pay for tuition, room and board, plus two trips to see us annually. With home leaves to the States each summer, we would see him then as well. We were anxious at first, but it turned out to be a wonderful solution!

Another family related:

> We had lived in Brussels for two and a half years. Sharon was half-way through her junior year in high school when our company asked us to move to Brazil. Rather than have our daughter go through the trauma of entering a new school, making all new friends and coping with the culture shock of a new country, we decided to have her return to our hometown and live with her married brother's family and finish high school with her old friends and where she had grown up.

A third educational option, mentioned previously in this book, is the possibility of home study courses. For some, this has proven to be an excellent alternative to repatriating or separating the family. If this is of interest, you will want to analyze the programs thoroughly, and make sure they fulfill the long-range objectives for your child. Do these programs offer a broad or focused curriculum and, if your children are college bound, are the home study courses properly accredited? Expatriate families have used home study programs all over the world and for various grade levels. Some maintain that the overall education gained from remaining abroad far outweighs the lack of a classroom environment.

Adapting the New to the Old

For the majority of expatriates, repatriation is an exciting and happy prospect. Repatriation represents the termination and completion of the family's adventure abroad, and the resumption of life in a familiar environment. Their foreign experiences are treasured memories, and there is a warmth and comfort associated with "moving home." The closeness of the family, the renewing of old friendships, the excitement of learning first hand what's new and different are all part of the transition. The opportunity to communicate, share and build upon what the expatriate family has experienced is an exhilarating thought. Repatriation is the start of a new beginning.

Making the Move

Now that the decision has been made to "move home," and you know generally what to expect, let's get on with the move. Since you should consider your repatriation as you would another international move, you may want to return to the beginning of this book and reread it. Start by determining why you are moving, as the answer may impact your initial decisions. For example, if your spouse has received a significant promotion, are you likely to be doing a lot more entertaining in the future? If so, you might want to forego the idea of that cute little house for one with substantially more open space. Or, if your repatriation is due to a major corporate reorganization, you may want to consider renting rather than buying a house until the dust settles.

As strange as it may sound, research where you are going. Although the majority of people repatriate to the general area where they lived prior to moving abroad, this does not mean that you must live in your old hometown. In fact, you have a unique opportunity to examine other towns or cities, their school systems, their qualities of life, and other factors that are important to your current needs. Our survey results showed that over half of repatriated expatriates opted to relocate to communities other than those they left.

Finally, determine when the move should take place. It is possible the family may not want to move at the same time as the spouse-employee. The employer may need the employee in his new assignment immediately. However, if it is the middle of the school year, it may be advisable for the family to postpone its departure. Conversely, the family might find itself preceding the spouse-employee's repatriation. For example, one lady told us:

> We learned in July that the company wanted us to return to the States in October. Since school was out and our house in New Jersey was vacant, we decided that the kids and I would leave almost immediately. We packed our household goods, called in the movers and took off on a month's trip. We timed our arrival home to coincide with the movers. My husband returned to Cairo, where he rented a small flat, and spent the remaining two months putting his corporate affairs in order. It was one of the easiest moves we ever made.

As you are planning your repatriation, it is time to start making lists again. For starters, make sure to cover the following items:

—Why are we moving? Any special considerations?
—When will we move? Any timing considerations?
—What visas, permits, etc., will be needed?
—What can/cannot be taken back to the States?
—What are the border and customs requirements?
—How will we move: land, air or sea?
—Who will pack, move and unpack us?
—Where will we be living? What are our options?
—Special educational considerations when we arrive?
—Social, cultural, recreational opportunities?
—Any health or security issues?
—Career opportunities or consideration?

And make a list of what you will need to:

—Buy before you leave;
—Sell rather than ship;
—Give away rather than keep;
—Discontinue (leases), change (phone, electrical, etc.), or cancel (memberships);
—Notify (household help, schools, churches, clubs, U.S. embassy);
—Arrange for necessary exit permits, customs declarations, and health documentation for family and pets;
—Obtain copies of legal documents (marriage, divorce, adoption) that you may have obtained while living abroad. (These documents, as well as school transcripts and medical records, should be hand-carried to ensure their safety.)

Don't forget to involve your spouse and children in the

preparation of your lists. They have obligations and responsibilities, as well. As with your international sojourn, you can set the emotional tone for your family's repatriation. Involve your spouse and children in the plans for the move. They, more than likely, will have places they want to visit "one last time," friends and commitments that require last-minute attention, and mementos to purchase. Everyone always has "something special" they want to take home for their "memory bank." It will help each person's transition if they can participate and feel they've fulfilled their individual goals.

It's also a good time to create an air of celebration. Keep a happy tone. "Hasn't this been a great experience, and isn't it neat we can now share it with all our family and friends?" This will go a long way to dispel the feelings of sadness associated with moving.

Plan parties and events to help ease the transition for everyone in the family. Though, here, we would like to add a word of caution. It is quite common for parents to get caught up in the plethora of move preparations, their own farewell parties, and to forget that this is a natural part of "moving-on" for everyone, including the children. Let each child decide how he or she wants to handle their departure. Make sure every event is happy and upbeat. Encourage the kids to swap photos and addresses with their close friends and to plan future visits. As one mother told us:

When it came time for us to return to the U.S., everyone was happy except our thirteen year old. She was "in love," and no matter what we said or did, she felt her life was over. As a last resort, I suggested she invite the "young man" to spend part of the summer with us in the States. It was December at the time, and June was a long way off. As spring approached, she made the transition to her new life and, as expected, a "new love" appeared on the scene.

Another mother told us:

> We moved back to the States when both of our boys were still in elementary school. I could see that they were sad and apprehensive about the move. So, my husband and I worked together to make this a "great adventure." We had them plan parties, do a "scavenger hunt" collecting information on our host country to share at their new school, and build models of the plane they would fly home on. We continued our "adventure" when we got back to the States, making our hotel time seem like a vacation and "camping-out" in our new home for a week. We worked together to pick out colors for each child's room, and celebrated with a "house warming" party when each was unpacked and decorated. We brought back regulation soccer goal cages and word spread like wild-fire that our backyard was now the official field for neighborhood games.

For the most part, expatriate women found repatriation very similar to previous moves, with most of the same highs and lows. As with all transitions, it takes time to settle everyone in and reestablish their feeling of belonging and of being in-step with their surroundings. It was generally agreed that, within a year the repatriated family says, "This is our home." By then, the waves of "reverse culture shock" have ebbed and life has moved on.

We mentioned at the beginning of this book that your expatriate experience would make you grow and change. You are probably not even aware of many of these transformations, as they occurred slowly and subtly. However, if you reflect on all of the events that led up to this point in your life, you will probably find much in common with those who have made their expatriate experience a success. More than likely, you started with a positive attitude and were optimistic and open-minded as you went along. Your ability to accept and deal with change—and your sense of humor—stood you in good stead. These traits, coupled with your new knowledge, has most certainly given you a greater understanding and respect for the world around you. Every experience you have had has now made you a stronger and better person. More than likely, you have proved to be a valuable asset to your spouse and the corporation. Your self-satisfaction and personal fulfillment are well earned and well deserved.

Congratulations and all the best with your next adventure!

Especially for Husbands

*The keys to being a successful international husband
are awareness and sensitivity. Adaptation of the family is
a Number One priority. As such, it deserves as much time
and attention on the husband's part as any other aspect of
the new responsibilities abroad.*

A MAJOR THEME OF THIS HANDBOOK has been how important it is for companies to recognize the critical role
performed by their employee's spouse and why it's essential they assure her successful adaptation to international
life. She is the cornerstone of a supportive home life and
the linchpin of the family unit. If she succeeds, chances
are greatly enhanced their employee will succeed.

It is even more important that husbands recognize
these same dynamics and accept their responsibility to
help their wives succeed. To do any less would jeopardize
the husband's career and the family's happiness and well-
being. With forethought and sensitivity, there is much a

husband can and should do to enable his wife to perform her role effectively.

The Decision

A husband's responsibility to assist his wife begins well before his line, "I've got something to tell you . . . the company has offered me a position overseas." The decision to move abroad is usually a momentous one for the family. Recognizing this fact, a wise husband will have thought through the decision-making process he is about to initiate.

The first stage, that of broaching the subject, is probably the most traumatic. His wife's initial response will probably be, "Where? When? What's it like?" and "What about the children?" "And what about my career?" It's very reassuring if her spouse has anticipated these concerns. It is important that this exchange be as objective and unemotional as possible. It's equally important that the discussion be a dialogue, not a sales pitch or dictum. The wife must be a participant in the decision. Participation leads to commitment; and a wife's commitment to the decision—to move or not—is essential.

A second phase of the decision comes when husband and wife grapple with the more cerebral aspects of making such a dramatic change. "Is it right for your career?" "What repercussions will it have on our family?" "What are our other options and where would they lead?" Here forethought and preparation by the husband can be of major assistance to his wife. Contrast, for example, the husband who is prepared to discuss the philosophic and "career" aspects of the decision with the husband who rambles, unfocused and unprepared, while thinking out loud. It's the former who will be of most help in reaching a rational decision. Previous discussions with his supervisor, the personnel department, co-workers and other friends who have either the experience or the perspective will provide invaluable input.

If the husband's company offers a trip to the new location—either before or after the decision has been made—he should make the time to go himself and, if at all possible, take his wife.

At some point, it is essential that the decision be discussed with the children and other members of the family. Remember, it is important that they are a party to, and participants in, the process. The timing of these discussions will vary with the age and circumstances of all the family members; but these discussions cannot be left to the wife to handle in isolation. The husband must play a coequal role in managing the process. His enthusiasm, confidence, perspective, and broad shoulders are just as important to the children as they are to his wife. The husband can also play a meaningful role in reviewing the information provided by the company or by his own research and directing the family to appropriate resources, such as reference books or friends with overseas experience.

Last, a phase of the decision-making process, which may occur at any time, concerns questions regarding the "package" and the company's overseas policies. While some wives prefer to leave these issues to their husbands' best judgment, other wives appreciate knowing the details of compensation, allowances, perks, and the like. A thoughtful husband analyzes the package and discusses its pros and cons with his wife, comparing them to his current position and future prospects. Listen to what your wife has to say. She may be able to give you ideas that will result in a better compensation package for all concerned!

The Move

Once the decision has been taken to accept the company's offer of a position abroad, the work load and stress of actually moving typically fall on the shoulders of the wife. The multitude of details and the decisions that are made while the husband is absorbed in preparing for his new assignment are major subjects of this book.

There are numerous ways in which husbands can ease the burden of moving. First of all, reading *Moving and Living Abroad* from cover to cover, as opposed to this chapter alone, will provide the husband with an appreciation for the tremendous amount of work involved. In some cases, husbands can assume primary responsibility, such as in arranging for insurance. In other cases, a husband's involvement is optional, such as in helping to pack household belongings. For the first move abroad, we suggest that each husband get as deeply involved as his schedule permits, particularly if his wife is winding down her own career. After the second or third move, it will be clear where a husband can contribute and where he simply adds to the chaos. As one husband admitted candidly:

> After our third move, I finally figured it out. As moving day approached, I would make myself scarce . . . pushing papers at the office. If my wife needed help, I would hear about it. Previously, whenever I tried to assist, I found myself underfoot and was obviously more of a hindrance than a help.

When and where should husbands assist with the move? Our suggestions would be:

—Determining company policies and procedures;

—Negotiating any special requests;

—Deciding whether to rent or sell your house;

—Selecting the mover, negotiating price, and arranging for insurance;

—Organizing work papers, import permits, and any legal matters;

—Arranging pre-move briefings; organizing travel plans, tickets, passports, visas, and hotels.

Those jobs for which a husband's assistance is optional include:

—Shopping for transformers, 220-volt appliances, and other last minute items;

—Deciding what to ship, store, and sell;

—Recording and valuing the household inventory;

—Managing the mover (timing, special services, packing materials, etc.);

—Obtaining passports, visas, and shots;

—Notifying others of your move (banks, insurance companies, subscriptions, schools);

—Arranging for mail forwarding.

Settling In

Once you've arrived, the task of settling in begins in earnest. If the company hasn't provided you with a place to live, the first chore will be locating a house or apartment. While wives typically make the rounds with the realtor, there are a number of areas where husbands can assist. These include: selecting reputable real estate agents, providing a car and driver for the search, determining most suitable locations, assisting with the final selection, and negotiating the terms of a lease.

Once the furniture arrives, unpacking can be an onerous task if a wife tries to accomplish it single handedly. A husband's strong arms and back at this point, as well as his time commitment, are much appreciated contributions. Even the mundane task of acting as a "gofer" is a great help.

Be Sensitive, Be Supportive, Be a Hero

One of the most important contributions a husband can make is to act as a cheerleader for his wife. Be supportive, no matter what! Restrain yourself from saying, "Why on earth did you . . .?" Listen patiently and be a good sounding board.

Husbands can also plan ahead for the end of each day. Take your wife out to dinner or bring it in with champagne and flowers. Make sure to arrange for a quiet moment for just the two of you. It will do wonders to recharge your mental batteries and enthusiasm to forge ahead. Special, unanticipated gestures—like making an appointment to have her hair done and a manicure at the hotel beauty salon—are simple but long-remembered tokens of appreciation. Other suggestions include:

—Hire bilingual help for the settling-in period,
—Arrange for someone to look after and entertain the children,
—Engage a tutor to provide the family with a few quick language lessons,
—Hire a local handyman on a per hour basis,
—Arrange for a driver for a couple of weeks,
—Contract for the heavy-duty cleaning chores before the furniture arrives,
—Order stationery with your new address,

—Send out change of address notices,
—Have potted plants and/or fresh flowers delivered to
  the house.

The First Six Months

The most critical time in any international move is the
first six months in the new location. This is the period
when the family will confront and cope with the physical
aspects of the move, the emotional trauma of relocation,
and the experience of culture shock. This is the window
of time during which a husband has the greatest opportunity to make a significant impact on the family's successful adaptation to the new home. Anticipation, recog-
nition, and comprehension of the family's needs, both
physical and emotional, are key elements to achieving
this. Rather than simply hoping that everyone will adjust
with the passage of time, a husband should tackle the situation head on. Examples include:

—Be sensitive to your wife's moods and signals, antic-
  ipating when she needs you and when she is best left
  to do the job on her own;
—Be sensitive to your children's feelings and needs, as
  well;
—Plan trips to resorts and places of interest during holiday periods or school vacations;
—Bring back small gifts and presents after long business trips away from home;
—Remember anniversaries, birthdays, and the like;
—Organize family outings, recreation, and events
  which bring the family together;
—Or, as one husband did so thoughtfully when he re-

turned from a business trip to the States at Thanksgiving time, carry a frozen turkey in your tote bag.

Moving On and Moving Home

The time will come, once again, when you utter those memorable words, "I've got something to tell you . . . we're moving." Whether you're moving on to another international location or moving home, keep in mind that each move is different. While practice makes almost perfect, no two relocations are the same. Each has its own set of unique circumstances and problems. Rereading this handbook will serve as a good reminder, providing focus to the task at hand and a memory jog as to what lies ahead. It will also bring back memories of *who* performed what tasks effectively and, in particular, where a husband's contribution was most appreciated.

If the family is thrilled at the prospect of moving on or returning home, a husband's role in assuring the family's adjustment is relatively simple. If, however, a wife or the children are not ready for the move, the dynamics of "the decision" are at hand again. Our advice here is to draw on your past experiences and the lessons you learned from your last move. Treat the move as you would any other and rely on your instincts to arrive at the proper decision.

As with most moves, your prime concern may be your children's readjustment. According to many well traveled husbands, a key consideration is the community into which you move. They suggest: be flexible as to the amount of time you allow for driving to work, so that you can put your family's needs on a par with your own; look for schools that suit the needs of your children, remain sensitive to emotional needs and loss of personal support systems.

As one father related:

When we returned to the States, we chose our house because of the neighborhood. There were kids all over the place. Our children could ride their bikes to school and get a game of football started in the backyard at the drop of a hat. Our children were starved for playmates and the close promixity of friends. After eight years of living behind walls in our villa and under constant adult supervision, they needed the proximity of their peers and the freedom of being able to go out and find new friends.

Once the decision of where to live is made, it is important to be sensitive to the emergence of peer group pressure. Certain styles and brand names may be really important to your children. Be aware of this and save the lectures on "family thrift" until everyone is settled in, feels comfortable, and has restarted the new life.

Contributing to your children's sense of self-worth is an important investment of time and energy. Encourage them to continue to utilize the talents and skills they gained from living overseas. If your child is an accomplished soccer player and the new school doesn't have a team, you may want to get one started. If he or she has learned the rudiments of a foreign language, encourage its continued study.

Last, but definitely not least by any means, it is imperative that a husband consider the adjustment needs of his wife. He will probably be getting a promotion with his transfer. His wife, on the other hand, may be losing her household help and returning to work. Help your wife to recognize the value of her overseas experience, both personally and professionally. If reentry to the work force suits her interests, explore the possibilities of how she might leverage her overseas experience. Whether or not she turns to a career outside the home, now is the time for you to change roles. Be her sounding board and help her to explore her options. You are one of the few people who know exactly how much she has changed and grown, and how very much she has to offer to the surrounding business and social communities.

Index